Becoming an Intentional Woman of God

Nancy Wheat

ISBN: 979-8-7178-4706-3

Foreword

Nancy Wheat, the author of this book, is my aunt, my dad's sister. If you're not sure you've met her, *you haven't met her*. She's unforgettable: warm, outgoing, hospitable, and a natural leader. She has a beautiful voice, a compassionate heart, and a thirst for spiritual matters.

Nancy has been more than just an aunt to me. She has been a Barnabas, a second mom, and a mentor in ministry. She is genuine. She is imperfect. She is a friend.

This book of hers has been "brewing" a long time. I have heard many portions of it verbally – over countless phone calls, texts of encouragement, and cups of tea. I have also pored over its pages, with tears slipping down my face because I needed the grace, wisdom, and experience that can only be passed from an older woman to a younger woman (Titus 2:3-5). I can tell you honestly that I have needed to hear her words and that God has used them to help my heart.

But I am not alone in this scenario – there are many other women, both young and "more mature," who have been blessed to share such time with Nancy (and her tea!). This book is simply one long cuppa with her – a piece of her heart, her godly wisdom and her own experience, passed to you, on paper instead of with the warm press of her hand.

So, go brew that cup of tea (or coffee) and sit down to listen as Nancy speaks to each of our hearts. May we all be challenged to live more intentionally, more selflessly, *more like Jesus* because of it.

God's richest blessings,
Tracy (Mitchell) Watts

Contents

Introduction

Why write a book about intentional women you ask? I have spent many hours listening to tearful, frustrated and discouraged preacher's wives pour their hearts out. Women who honestly want to serve God but have such a load on their shoulders feel immobilized.

These women bear a burden of unrealistic and even unbiblical expectations. I want this book to be one that will help lift that load. I hope to present a biblical "expectation"; I want to honor and praise these sisters for the hard role they fill so very well. Then, having been a preacher's wife for over thirty years, I hope to add some tips, stories and advice that will help them to be God's person in their unique spot.

The struggle to find how God wants us to fit in the kingdom does not just occur with preacher's wives, however. I find that many women don't know what God has gifted them to do. So, this book is for all Christian women. I pray all women will find things in this book to enable them to shine for Jesus. I hope to talk about how we can strengthen ourselves spiritually so that we can take Satan on in life's spiritual battle.

I will cover topics such as spiritual nutrition, marriage, parenting, mission work, hospitality, and how to remain content. I have also asked many female leaders to share with me their advice, their heartaches, their victories and their heroines' stories. These are women whose walk I admire and try to emulate - not perfect women but ones who know that the power is God's and that whatever we do we do only because He enables us.

I pray that women will leave the reading of this book better prepared to keep on keeping on. I hope to do what Hebrews 10:24 tells us to: "Let us consider how to stir up one another to love and good works."

My prayer is that this book will help us all be the women God intended us to be. Becoming this woman doesn't just "happen." We won't drift into being godly women. It has to be intentional, and so I give you this book of what I have gleaned from 60 years of living, the wisdom of my heroines of faith and most importantly God's precious love letter to us in His word. There can be no better manual for the intentional Christian woman.

Chapter 1: Be Yourself

There seems to be an unwritten list of what a preacher's wife should be like. Where do we get this list from? Certainly not from God. There is no list of qualifications or even a description of duties for a preacher's wife in God's word. But we the church have this list. How many times have you heard people say, "that's not how a preacher's wife should be," "she isn't much of a preacher's wife," or "why isn't the preacher's wife doing that?" Perhaps you haven't said those exact words, but we have certainly thought them, or something like them.

When we allow our church family to dictate what we should be like, we are giving them authority that only God has. The authority to bind something like this is God's alone.

So, you might ask, "How can I prepare to be a preacher's wife?" Or perhaps, "How can I be a better preacher's wife?" Maybe that's the wrong question. Since God did not leave us a job description for a preacher's wife or a list of qualifications, we should ask instead "how can I be a Christian woman?" The fact that I am married to a preacher will give me a different set of opportunities and challenges, but it does not change the fact that God has given me a charge to be His woman no matter who I am married to. There are direct commands given to me as a Christian, as a Christian woman, as a wife, and as a mother, commands given to me to use my unique, God given talents in His kingdom.

1 Peter 2.9

Psalm 139

How do I become an intentional Christian woman then? The first thing I tell these sisters to do is to "be yourself." This is the advice every individual needs when struggling with the demands of a role they are cast in. When we try to be someone we are not, we will eventually fall flat on our faces. We will stay extremely frustrated and therefore function at less than our best.

rejoice in who God made you to be.

Of course, in order to be yourself you have to know yourself. This often takes years to fully learn, but even as a young woman I knew what I was best suited for and what was not the real, authentic me. Learning to listen to gut feelings about who we are may be hard at first. We may have to ask for help from close friends or family who know and love us. We also need to spend much time in prayer. Pray that God will help us use what He has already gifted us for.

1

My mom was a preacher's wife. She was by nature a very quiet, even shy person. She preferred not to be in the limelight. Yet, she was a marvelous servant of God who labored in the kingdom powerfully because she knew herself and did not try to be someone else or someone else's idea of who she should be. I was blessed to be raised by a woman who applied this principle not just to herself but also to others. She did not try to make her "loves to be in the middle of the room" daughter a quiet, behind the scenes person. In fact, she seemed amazed and proud of the gifts she could see God developing in me. We need to give each other this kind of support and appreciation as we explore our individual gifts.

Sometimes we are very hard on one another. We have hugely unrealistic expectations of each other. We need to repent of this and look in the mirror of God's word to see our own reflection. In Hamlet, Shakespeare said "This above all: to thine own self be true/ And it must follow, as the night the day, thou canst not be false to any man" (Act I Scene III).

I Peter 4:10-11 tells us "As each has received a gift, use it to serve one another, as good stewards of God's varied grace: whoever speaks, as one who speaks oracles of God; whoever serves, as one who serves by the strength that God supplies—in order that in everything God may be glorified through Jesus Christ. To him belong glory and dominion forever and ever. Amen." We glorify God by using our individual gifts. We glorify Him by being who He made us to be.

Romans 12:4-8 is even more specific: "For as in one body we have many members, and the members do not all have the same function, so we, though many, are one body in Christ, and individually members one of another. Having gifts that differ according to the grace given to us, let us use them: if prophecy, in proportion to our faith; if service, in our serving; the one who teaches, in his teaching; the one who exhorts, in his exhortation; the one who contributes, in generosity; the one who leads, with zeal; the one who does acts of mercy, with cheerfulness." What a beautiful picture of God's body being made up of all kinds of gifted people. We have to figure out what we are gifted with and then decide how that will be used in our church family.

Several years ago, a young preacher's wife came to my house to ask for help with her new role. She was surprised to find herself there because she had not married a preacher. He had decided to preach some years into their marriage. She was not mentally or emotionally prepared. She felt like others were expecting a certain kind of preacher's wife, one that she felt she could never be.

The first thing I told her was "just be yourself." She was relieved to hear someone say this but nervous at first about how then to fit into the work of the body of the church. As we talked, I believe she became more comfortable and felt like this approach made sense.

It does make sense because our Lord did not make a mistake when He made us all with different abilities and skills. He knew the church needed many things to be done and if we were all the same, those things would not be completed. I Corinthians 12:18-20 confirms this: "But as it is, God arranged the members in the body, each one of them, as he chose. If all were a single member, where would the body be? As it is, there are many parts, yet one body." The fact that God arranged us as multi-functional should fill us with a deep joy and sense of affirmation.

You are exactly where you are supposed to be.

Since God made us with unique gifts, He also expects us to use them. Romans 12:6 tells us "having gifts that differ according to the grace given to us, let us use them." That is always the tricky part with us Christians. We forget to use what God gives us, or we simply choose not to use what He gave us.

We need to decide what gifts God has given us. We will have to ignore what others think we need to do and do, instead, what God has gifted us to do. Then we need to get busy using those precious gifts. I often think of the parable of the talents in Matthew 25:14-30 when I think of how God expects us to use whatever He has given us to serve Him. The servant who had one talent and hid it in the ground was called "slothful" (Matthew 25:36). Then God says "For to everyone who has will more be given, and he will have an abundance. But from the one who has not, even what he has will be taken away" (Matthew 25:29). Our father has entrusted us with these precious abilities. Preacher's wife, schoolteacher, homemaker, nurse, doctor: He expects us to use what He gave us.

use it or lose it.

If you really don't know what your gift is, ask for help. Ask God first and then ask wise people who know and love you. Proverbs 11:14 (NIV) says, "Where there is no guidance, a people falls, but in abundance of counselors there is safety." Some of the worst decisions my husband and I have made in our ministry have been ones made without seeking guidance from those who have more experience and wisdom, those who maybe just have a little different

Prov. 15:2

3

perspective than we had at the time. Sometimes we are too close to see what our real abilities are and those who know us and love us can help us appropriate them.

Seeking wise advice is very different from allowing every random person in our congregation to tell us who we are supposed to be. Choose individuals who have proven they have your best interests at heart and those who have shown they have spiritual and emotional maturity.

Studying the women of the Bible helps us to see how God does really love variety. God has always used a variety of "types" to accomplish His mission: Sarah was brave and willing to follow her husband without knowing where in the world they were going. She managed a huge household and did it from a tent. Deborah was willing to go into battle with a less than perfect, weak male leader, who she challenged to step up to leadership. Esther was a quiet, tactful, prayerful, submissive woman who saved her people from extinction. Ruth was hard working and obedient to her mother-in-law, and God blessed that submission by including her in the lineage of Jesus. Dorcas was a great seamstress and showed love by what she made for others. Lydia was hospitable from the day she was baptized. Priscilla taught alongside her husband, a kind and considerate woman who did not want to belittle Apollos but taught him privately. Mary was chosen by God to raise His own son.... The list could go on. Studying the gifts of Godly women in the Bible can really help you find your own gift, as well as affirm your faith and service.

Trusting that God did not make a mistake in the way He made you is a wonderful expression of faith. Don't compare yourself to others; only compare yourself to God. Don't envy others' abilities; rejoice with them in how God made them to serve. Accept that God has a place for you and your sisters in the body of Christ. Really learn to see the family of God as a body that needs every part to work at optimum strength.

As a teen I was privileged to be able to watch a lovely group of missionary wives work together as a team. Each one came to the field with very different gifts. They knew how to cheer each other on. Betty was a wonderful public speaker, fearless in her teaching, a marvelous southern cook and a surrogate mom to so many. My mom was a gentle, quiet teacher opening her home to my crowds of noisy friends. She was good at encouraging us all with small words of praise, a great cook, and unflappable. Kay was a super visual aid maker, great children's teacher, and especially good with teaching kids to memorize God's word in fun ways. She was a great example as a young mom and willing to live in the village areas with her husband and children during extended periods that the preaching school students did their practical training. Sharon was stylish, young, and very good at talking to us teens about purity, love, and friendship. Rita was English and very direct with those she taught one on one and publicly. She made great chips (French fries) and opened her home to us young people. Louise was excellent with babies and toddlers, opening their home to young families who needed her patient guidance. Each of these heroines had many other gifts I haven't listed but these stood out to me as gifts that they had realized and employed already by their twenties and thirties. Were they unsure of themselves? Did they get frustrated? I am sure they did, but they were unafraid to be themselves. They celebrated one another's differences truly using those different talents for God. We have to see that God gave us these gifts to be strong in the battle against sin and Satan.

Being yourself is often hard when faced with a congregation that thinks they know who you should be. How then do you meet this challenge? First, be strong in your determination to be yourself: the woman you really are. Ask for your husband's help to stand your ground when pushed to fill roles you are not comfortable with. In time you will find women in the church who will understand where you are coming from and they will help you. But at first you and your husband must be united.

This unity may start even during the interviewing process. Plan ahead with your husband. Prepare him to be able to say what you feel as a Christian woman you are called to do. This will help set the tone for your arrival and settling in. Plan good ways to present what you are willing to do. Be positive and firm when pressured by people once you are moved in. State what you are gifted and willing to do.

One of my favorite preacher's wives wrote me this "For those young wives who are just starting out and feel the eyes of the brethren on her to see how she will 'perform' – just be a Christian, the kind God will be proud of, and you will be the best preacher's wife you can be. The congregation is hiring your husband, not you."

The advice Paul gave the young preacher Timothy would be good for us as well: "…fan into flame the gift of God, which is in you through the laying on of my hands, for God gave us a spirit not of fear but of power and love and self-control" (2 Timothy 1:6-7). The NIV says He did not give us a spirit of timidity. In other words, be strong in who you are and what you are gifted to do. Respect yourself and others will treat you with respect. You are in fact giving God respect by this too.

Finally, remember that just as God had a plan for the children of Israel, He has one for you. He cares deeply about every one of His children. I love to think about what He said to Israel even while they were in captivity in Babylon. "For I know the plans I have for you, declares the Lord, 'plans for wholeness and not for evil, to give you a future and a hope. Then you will call upon me, and I will hear you. You will seek me and find me when you seek me with all your heart. I will be found by you declares the Lord..." (Jeremiah 29:11-14 NIV). He had a plan for the Jews even in captivity if they sought Him whole heartedly. He will help us too if we seek Him. We need to be who He planned for us to be.

I found this quote many years ago and I share it with you now: "What you are is God's gift to you. What you make of yourself is your gift to God." So, decide what your gift is, and then go be yourself!

Questions

1. Name some ways to keep from buying into others' ideas of what you as a preacher's wife or leader should be.
2. Make a list of gifts you possess that can be used in God's kingdom. If you struggle to do this, ask a friend who might see you with less critical eyes than you have for yourself.
3. Make a list of five women in the Bible whom you admire for their service to God. Write down what their gifts were and how they used those gifts.
4. Study the word 'envy' in the Bible. How does envy affect learning what role we play in the body?

1. Develop a game plan w/ my husband before going in. Have confidence that you are God's daughter + He loves you.

2. Bible teacher, decorator (bulletin boards, building singer (during worship, Kings Quartet)

3. · Ruth - quiet servant
· Esther - quiet bravery
· Deborah - leader, warrior
· Priscilla - teammate, teacher
· Mary (mother of Jesus) - God-fearing, trusting

4. Comparison is the thief of joy. It also blinds us to our own abilities. We spend too much time watching another woman "water her grass" that we forget/neglect/ complain about our own.

Chapter 2: Eat Your Veggies (Feeding Yourself Spiritually)

A dear friend of mine sent me this advice for preacher's wives. "This is God's work. Ministry will not replace the time I need to spend in the word or alone with God. Always put God first, family and then ministry." Priorities. Tough to keep straight aren't they? But we really must take seriously the need to keep ourselves spiritually nourished, or we will starve.

I was listening to a segment on National Public Radio a while ago. The subject was treatment for anorexia nervosa. It caught my attention because unlike approaches to treatment I had heard of in the past, this study showed that the most successful treatments were the ones where the patient is "force fed," not with a tube, but by family members sitting with the patient and coaxing the person to eat. They had to be "forced" to eat before they were ready to heal the emotional and mental issues that caused the disease.

I began to think about our spiritual diet. We are often anorexic spiritually speaking. Peter says, "like newborn infants, long for the pure spiritual milk, that by it you may grow up to salvation" (I Peter 2:2). We need to be like that, but that often goes against our natural desires. So how do we learn to crave that milk?

As with anorexia, drastic measures need to be taken to save our lives. Physically, we often have to train ourselves to crave healthy foods like broccoli, apples, spinach, etc. We may have to train ourselves to crave the spiritual spinach, broccoli and apples in our daily life as well. We might even have to quit some junk food in order to create a desire for what is healthy. We may have to "force feed" ourselves at first by making ourselves read God's word every day. Just as the body starts to long for good food when taught, our spiritual self will quickly crave and miss that spiritual food when not given it.

Once more this is something all Christian women need to be concerned about, not just women in ministry or whose husbands are in ministry. James 3:1 tells us that "Not many of you should become teachers, my brothers, for you know that we who teach will be judged with greater strictness." Any leadership position we take will put us in a position where others will look to us for example. This makes our spiritual nourishment even more crucial. We need excellent "food" to grow strong enough to withstand what the devil will throw at us.

What we love we spend time on. Who we love we spend time with. Do we really love God? Do we love His word? That should be seen by the amount of time we spend with Him and with His word. A young man who claims to love a girl finds every way to spend time with that girl. There is no doubt where his affections lie because his actions show us. Does God see how much I love Him by how much time I listen to Him?

Psalm 119:105 says, "Your word is a lamp to my feet and a light to my path." Is it really my light to see the path I am walking in? When I do not read His word, it is like I am refusing to turn the light on in a pitch-dark room. I will fall and stumble my way around.

"The lamp of the Lord searches the spirit of man; it searches out his inmost being" (Proverbs 20:27 NIV). When I read and apply His word, it searches my spirit. God's word sees deeply into my heart; my motives are laid bare. It guides, cleanses and purifies. It corrects me. Proverbs 6:23 says, "For the commandment is a lamp and the teaching a light, and the reproofs of discipline are the way of life." Discipline from God: What a blessing! When I am constantly reading His word, I will find the discipline from God easier to receive and grow from.

Do you need help having good judgment? I do. We find that in God's word, too. Psalm. 119:66-68 says, "Teach me good judgment and knowledge, for I believe in your commandments. Before I was afflicted I went astray, but now I keep your word. You are good and do good; teach me your statutes." In ministry and in life, we are constantly in situations where good judgement is needed. If we are deeply studying the word, asking Him to give us knowledge and judgement, He will not fail us. Our daily cry should be like the psalmist's: "teach me your statutes." Maybe we should read two or three verses every day from Psalm 119 as the theme of that Psalm has to do with what His statutes bring us when we keep them in our hearts.

To eat right is a choice. I have the ability to make a choice to eat right spiritually too. Proverbs 12:1 says, "Whoever loves discipline loves knowledge, but he who hates reproof is stupid." That says it quite bluntly. Don't be stupid. Be wise. Love knowing God's word.

We need to be zealous, passionate people but people with knowledge. Good food makes us strong and healthy. Consumption of God's food will likewise make us strong and healthy Christians. I often wonder what Paul would say to me in regard to my spiritual diet. I Cor 3:1-3 says, "But I, brothers, could not address you as spiritual people, but as people of the flesh, as infants in Christ. I fed you with milk, not solid food, for you were not ready for it. And even now you are not yet ready, for you are still of the flesh." Would he call me an infant in Christ like he did the Corinthians? Would he have to say that I was not ready for solid food? Would he say, 'Grow up'? Instead, I pray we are women who "hunger and thirst" for the word, as described in Matthew 5:6. Or perhaps like the deer in Psalm 42:1. Can I honestly say, "As a deer pants for flowing streams, so pants my soul for you, O God"?

Again, we need to recall how the anorexic person got better. She had to eat even before her body wanted to. We will have to "eat" the word and get into the habit of hearing it before we will really crave it. After World War II many emaciated prisoners from the death camps had to learn to eat again. Their bodies no longer craved food; their bodies were actually eating themselves for sustenance. We cannot be like that spiritually, depending on ourselves for strength. We must feed on the word God gave us to build our spiritual bodies.

Here are some personal benefits of eating well. We will be stronger in our personal faith, and we will then have courage to share our faith with those around us (I Peter 3:15). We will have the strength to help those weaker than we are. Like the one trying to save a drowning person, we first must put on our own life vest. We need to be strong so that we can help draw others to Christ. We need to be near our God who loves us deeply.

Jesus told Peter his job was to "feed my lambs" (John 21:15). We are not apostles, but we are much like Peter. We have been thrust into a leadership position. James 3:1 warns us that as teachers we will be judged more strictly: "Not many of you should become teachers, my brothers, for you know that we who teach will be judged with greater strictness."

Our example must be the best it can be and the responsibility to guide souls is a fearful one. As leaders we need wisdom and knowledge. Just as Solomon prayed and asked God for wisdom, we need to ask God to lead us: "Give me now wisdom and knowledge to go out and come in before this people, for who can govern this people of yours" (2 Chronicles 1:10). We are not royalty in the same sense as Solomon but our job as leaders is just as important - maybe more. We need to pray for help to remain nourished so that we can lead wisely.

Proverbs 15:7 says, "the lips of the wise spread knowledge; not so the hearts of fools." Our lips will be wise if we fill ourselves with knowledge of God. We don't want to have the heart of a fool. We don't want to be foolish in leading and teaching. There is no way to overemphasize the importance of teaching and leading.

Malachi 2:7-9 is a message God gave the priests, but the warning is apt for us as leaders too: "For the lips of a priest should guard knowledge and people should seek instruction from his mouth, for he is the messenger of the Lord of hosts. But you have turned aside from the way. You have caused many to stumble by your instruction. You have corrupted the covenant of Levi, says the Lord of hosts, and so I make you despised and abased before all the people, inasmuch as you do not keep my ways but show partiality in your instruction." This passage describes what an awe-inspiring responsibility we have and how dire the consequences are if we are not the leaders we should be. We certainly don't want to be like the sons of Eli and Samuel.

Instead, we should try to be tactful like Aquila and Priscilla. Acts 18:26 tells us that "they took him aside and explained to him the way of God more accurately." We must also be humble like Apollos who "was an eloquent man, competent in the scriptures. He had been instructed in the way of the Lord. And being fervent in spirit he spoke and taught accurately the things concerning Jesus" (Acts 18:24b-25). These three individuals had a great passion to teach, and they were willing to learn from each other. Are we willing to let the word, as well as brothers and sisters, help us be able to know the word better?

Some may wonder how to implement this good eating plan. Here are some practical ideas:
- Make sure you choose a plan that you will stick with.
- Be disciplined about it. Choose a specific time every day and make yourself accountable to that time. Find a mentor if you struggle with this.
- Choose different ways of reading every year so that you don't become bored. Even good healthy food is more inviting when prepared in a variety of ways.

There are many online reading plans, one-year bibles, chronological bibles, and study guides. Consider your own personality and study style. Choose a way that helps you. The bible is on cd; listen to it. Make notes or keep a journal. Use a women's bible class book and work through it on your own. We are so very blessed to have so many resources. There is no excuse not to eat well and interestingly. Ask a strong Christian woman how she keeps her "diet" if you want more ideas.

In Zimbabwe the average village church may have three Bibles. In our home we probably have ten to fifteen! We are so blessed with so much good "food" at our fingertips, yet we starve ourselves. What would those Zimbabwean Christians give to have so many options? They would be eating a daily healthy diet! We must do the same as preacher's wives and leaders. Discouragement is the devil's favorite weapon. Don't let him keep you from nourishing yourself every day. Say instead, with the psalmist, "Oh how I love your law! It is my meditation all the day" (Psalm 119:97).

We women need time alone to do as Hannah did in 1 Samuel 1:15. She told Eli, "I was pouring out my soul to the Lord." We need to take the time to "ponder" the ways of God as Mary did (Luke 2:19). Our devotional lives should be the foundation and prerequisite to the other dimensions of our lives. Most older women will tell us that they wish they had spent more time in prayer, reading and meditating. The time you do this will depend on your body clock – whether you are a night owl or morning bird. So, does your family know you have been with Christ?

Questions

1. Name ten ways the word of God is described in Psalm 119.
2. Read 2 Timothy 3:16-17. Pray about the areas you need to be allowing scripture to reshape you.
3. Ask other Christians how they discipline themselves to read the Bible. Try a new approach that might help you hunger and thirst for the pure word of God.

Chapter 3: The Young Preacher's Wife

When I first got married, I was a young preacher's wife. Young implies "beginner." So, I was a beginner wife. I was very blessed to have seen a good example in my mother of what a wife should be. I say wife and not preacher's wife because what I observed was an example of how any wife should be with her husband. My husband being in such a visible leadership role put added pressure on me, but the basic wife role is the same for any Christian woman.

Why did God make woman? Did God ever make anything without a purpose or reason? Our God is a great creator; He has made every creature, minute to enormous, with a wonderful purpose. So, too, was woman made with a wonderful God-given purpose. It doesn't matter what any person's idea of woman's purpose is. God's purpose is the purpose we must fulfill.

Genesis tells the story of God creating this incredible universe. Each plant, fly, bird and animal in this marvelous creation had a purpose. Man's purpose was to tend the Garden of Eden (Genesis 2:15). It was a seemingly idyllic situation, but God said, "It is not good for man to be alone. I will make a helper suitable for him" (Gen. 2:18). Perfect as it was, God saw that something was not good: It was not good for man to be alone. Then God performed yet another miracle: He made Adam's helper, woman. Man was not complete – creation was not complete – until God made woman. There is no one in creation like woman.

Genesis 2:23-24 says, "The man said 'This is now bone of my bones and flesh of my flesh; she shall be called woman because she was taken out of man.'" The text goes on to tell us that "for this reason a man will leave his father and mother and be united to his wife and they will become one flesh." Woman's purpose is to partner with man. God created man and woman to form a unit, a family, the most basic unit in society. We are to help each other in the smooth running of the family. Man and woman have different roles in this family. Just as God stayed in heaven while Jesus came to earth to fulfill their work, each having a different role, man and woman have unique roles to fulfill in the home.

Animals fulfill their God-given roles through instinct. Most of what we do as people, though, has to be learned. Ephesians 5:21-33 and I Peter 3:1-9 tell women to be submissive to their husbands. To be submissive means to lovingly defer to someone or to put yourself wholly at the disposal of someone.

I am humbled by the way Jesus submitted His will to His father's. "Though he was in the form of God did not count equality with God a thing to be grasped, but made himself nothing, taking the form of a servant, being born in the likeness of men. And being found in human form, he humbled himself by becoming obedient to the pint of death, even death on a cross" (Philippians 2:6-8). Submission does not infer weakness. Submission is quite the opposite. It takes great self-denial, and self-control to submit to someone, to put our needs last. Jesus did just that, giving us the perfect example of strength and humility. He obeyed His father. Jesus' submission to the Father was beautiful. When I submit to my husband, I obey our loving father. What a beautiful thing in the sight of God!

Submission is not easy. It is not natural. We naturally want to have our own way in life. When we enter marriage and want to follow God's design, we each will have to submit to God. Ephesians 5:15 tells us to "look carefully then how you walk, not as unwise but as wise." Paul then discusses how we should use our time, using it as wise people who try to understand God's will. We should not live in drunkenness and debauchery, but have lives so filled with the spirit that we want to sing psalms and hymns with thankful hearts (Ephesians 5:16-20). Then follows separate instructions to husbands and wives on their obligations in this sacred relationship. This section of scripture becomes very specific and practical for husband and wife. This is truly how we can "look carefully how we walk" (Ephesians 5:15).

How then do we become better Christian wives? How do we honor God in this way? This passage tells us plainly – put your husband first: "Wives submit to your own husbands, as to the Lord" (Ephesians 5:22). Second, we must respect and love him: "Let the wife see that she respects her husband" (Ephesians 5:33b). It is interesting to me that God knew we might have trouble as ladies showing respect to our husbands. Pray together with your husband that you both can fulfill what God intended for your roles to be. There is just something very positive and motivating about praying about something this difficult. When we know each of us is praying and working on our relationship, it is so much easier to defeat Satan, who wants our marriages to fail. When these positions are out of order, we are in serious trouble. The father is emasculated and humiliated, the mother is frustrated, and the children are not content but rather are insecure. God's order has both sense and balance.

If we truly trust that God is in control of our lives and that He is leading us where He wants us to be, then we will be proud to be the "wife of a preacher." We will be willing to work side by side with him. We were never in any doubt as kids that dad came first in mom's eyes. Not that we were neglected in any way or unloved. She and dad were at the center of the family and we were the circle around our parents. Too often I see families where the kids come first. This makes them think the world revolves around them

Habits of life are set when we are young. Put your husband first from the very beginning of your marriage. Find an older woman whom you respect and admire for the way she loves her husband and children. One of my wise fellow preachers' wives sent me this advice: "For the younger I would say, 'Do not neglect your children for the sake of the brethren.' If you lose your children, then you will not have a good influence on those you are trying to reach. For the older— after the children have left the home, then you have a lot of time to mentor the younger. But never neglect your husband." This sweet lady and her husband have been married over fifty years and are still holding hands and verbally affirming one another. I love being around them just to remind me how to lift my husband up with words of praise and admiration, as well as with my body language.

"Never neglect your husband." How I wish I could shout that advice to all of us! My husband and I are always amazed and deeply saddened to spend time with friends who have forgotten that they chose one another, that they promised to love and honor one another, and that they committed their lives together in the presence of God. They made that sacred vow and have now let time, dullness, lack of effort and attention rob them of God's most wonderful earthly relationship.

Please, sisters, if you have any staleness or troubles in your marriage, stop everything and repair it. There are so many verses about marriage being precious. Proverbs 5:15-19 (NIV) says, "Drink water from your own cistern, running water from your own well, Should your springs overflow in the streets, your streams of water in the public squares? Let them be yours alone, never to be shared with strangers.' May your fountain be blessed, and may you rejoice in the wife of your youth. A loving doe, a graceful deer— may her breasts satisfy you always, may you ever be captivated by her love.'"

What a beautiful poetic description of physical love! This is a bond that God planned for married people to enjoy. If you are not enjoying this part of your relationship, please get help. Today we have so much good information and good counseling that there is really no excuse to remain in a problem stage. Pray about your sex life. Then, make a plan to have time for each other. Get a babysitter or take a nap during the day so you can be ready to give yourself to your husband physically. It is vital to the long-term health of your relationship. He needs it, but you do too. Physically and emotionally sexual intimacy is very healthy and created by God. The best sex education we kids had growing up was watching mom and dad kiss, pat and hug. We also knew that their bedroom door was closed at certain times for a reason. In our current world where our children see sex in wrong situations on tv, movies, school, and everyday life, we need to show God's plan for sex even more.

"Let marriage be held in honor among all and let the marriage bed be undefiled" (Hebrews 13:4). <u>Our ministry will be stronger when people see a happy, healthy marriage</u>. We will protect our husbands and ourselves from sexual sin by providing a good place to express the desires God Himself placed within us. One of our teachers in college told us that the relationship he and his wife had after twenty-five years was far better than at year one. We all thought he really couldn't know what he was talking about! But now that we have been married over forty years, we know he is absolutely right. The longer you know each other, the more free you feel to ask for what you need sexually. God made sex this way, an exciting, continuing exploration.

Take the time to keep romance alive, sisters, because the dividends will be huge. Plan time every week for a "date." It might just be a cup of coffee or a Sonic burger. Your husband needs to know you still get excited about time spent with him. Don't hesitate to ask people to watch your kids so that you can do this. When Bobby (my husband) was in graduate school, our kids were two and four years old. I "kidnapped" him for the night. My sweet mother-in-law came and spent the night with the kids. I took Bobby out for dinner, but I had also packed a bag for us and booked a room at a hotel. So, we had almost 24 hours alone. He was very surprised, but I think was especially reassured that he still was number one in my heart. We both felt rejuvenated and reconnected by our time alone. We need that time to center our family periodically. Even while working in Zimbabwe, we were very blessed by my parents who often kept our kids so we could go spend time alone. Especially on the mission field where there are so many demands on your time, this is crucial to the health of your marriage.

My mom always encouraged me while raising our children to remember that there would be time for another career after our children left the home. It really helped me to know that someone so wise believed that staying home and training our children was both valuable and worthwhile. In fact, one of the constants in all the comments and advice I received from preachers' wives while writing this book is how vital training our children is.

One wife said this: "As a young preacher's wife, I struggled with the fact that I felt that I was not doing enough for the Lord because I was tied up with young children. This feeling of not doing enough for the Lord was something I wrestled with for quite a while. As the kids got older, the answer came to me. Our work is firstly the raising of our children in the Lord. If we don't do it, who will? The Bible indicates that the woman's work is her children. Titus 2:4-5 says, 'The older women are to train the younger women to love their husbands and children... to be busy at home, to be kind and subject to husbands.'" She went on with many good pieces of advice from her experience. She adds, "The mother is soldier, guard, doing her best to protect her children from the onslaught of the world. The young preacher's wife is no different. Her work is firstly that of her children and husband. I Tim. 2:15 says, 'But women will be saved through childbearing— if they continue in faith, love and holiness.'"

We need to affirm and help our young wives in this God given, vital job. The Lord's work is everywhere, but it is important to do the work that God created woman to do in her home and with her husband. Other work for the Lord should not replace this work. When the children are grown and gone, this work will be replaced with plenty more work for the Lord in other areas. Proverbs 22:6 reminds us to "Train up a child in the way he should go; even when he is old he will not depart from it."

If there was one thing I was able to say to young mothers, it would be to "stay home." This time with our children is so very short and yet so very important. No career advancement, no "thing" we might buy with the extra income could ever be more valuable than the opportunity to shape and mold the hearts and lives of the precious souls God has lent to us. I will say more about the specifics of that training in the next chapter but here I would beg you especially as preachers' wives whose lives can often be filled with the needs and pleas of others' problems to focus first on the souls God has given you.

As a young mom, these thoughts from Judy Miller were something I tried to keep in my mind and heart.

<u>If I Am Not at Home</u>

Who will tell my daughters that the prettiest thing about them is their expression, and the sweetest thing is their smile?

Who will teach my sons that the kind of companions they choose will play a large part in their character formation?

Who will be there to listen with the heart to all their problems, struggle and confusions?

Who will show my girls that being a homemaker, wife and mother is the very best career in the whole world?

Who will provide cleanliness, order and control?

Who will be there to cuddle and hug and gentle them if I do not?

Who will pour "honey" as well as milk upon the hearts of my children?

Who will praise them for successful achievement, for what good is the accomplishment when there is no one there to praise— too busy to care?

Who will read aloud to the children and teach them that words are fun and books can be their best friends?

Who will teach them to cook and sew and work with their hands?

Who will laugh at my children's antics and "cut up" with them when they feel like being silly?

Who will express love to their father in their presence, so that they will see that marriage is good and beautiful?

Who will comfort them in their sorrows and cry with them when they want to cry?

Who will help them, sit with them, stay by them when they are lonely, discouraged or ill?

Who will tuck them in at night and send them to bed with a kiss if I am not there?

Who will support them and build up their self-esteem in their growing up years?

Who will pick up after them, do their laundry, cook for them and
mend their clothes?
Who will show them life is like a song, if the song is not sung from
my lips?
Who will show them God and point them to the Heavenly Home?
Who will point out the daily miracles of their lives and teach them
each season is a season to be celebrated… if I am not at home?
~Judy Miller (Mother of ten children)

There is just no substitute for a mom. No school, club, scout
troop, babysitter or grandparent can ever replace a mom. Set an
example, pray with your children and for your children, and read
God's word. Let them see you reading it for yourself, as well as with
them. Start young, reading short portions straight from God's word
even when infants, as well as Bible story books. Memorize scripture
with them. We teach them the alphabet and their numbers and that
is good, but God's word is even more important. Listen to their
every word, be their best audience so that in later years when they
are surrounded by other influences, they will still turn to you. Use
those "teachable" moments. In order to use those moments, we
need to be with them.

Questions

1. What do you think Philippians 2:3-5 has to say to a wife?
2. Why did God make woman according to Genesis 2:23-24?
3. Write out your understanding of the word submission. Read Philippians 2:5-8 to see if your submission is like Jesus' submission to the father.
4. Is your husband fully aware he is number one in your life? Read Ephesians 5:21-33. List things you can do to help him know he is loved and respected.

Chapter 4: The Mom of Preacher's Kids

"Don't let your kids play with the preacher's kids." Ever heard that said? It may have been spoken in jest but with a sharp edge to it, nevertheless. Why do we have the cultural stereotype of the rotten minister's kid? It is not just within the church, but people of the world believe it too.

Personally, I think troubled and messed up preacher's kids are far less common than we are led to believe, as is true with many stereotypes. However, since there is that stereotype there must be some truth to it. We don't want our precious children to fit this "type."

As with preacher's wives, there is no list of special or different commands for preacher's kids. They do however need to be taught what all children in godly homes should be taught. Ephesians 6:1-3 says, "Children obey your parents in the Lord, for this is right. 'Honor your father and mother' (this is the first commandment with a promise), that it may go well with you and that you may live long in the land." Another great truism is found in Proverbs 22:6: "Train up a child in the way he should go; even when he is old he will not depart from it."

We must train our children to daily live vibrant lives for our Lord, not because they are the preacher's children and are somehow expected to live to a much higher standard than the people in the pews, but because they are God's children.

This will take a very intentional type of parenting. One of the best compliments my husband Bobby and I were ever given was by some missionaries teaching in a university in Zimbabwe. They told us that they were very impressed with how we were very "intentional" with our parenting. They observed that most of us have no "plan" for how we want our children raised. They said they could see we had a plan. Not that we were perfect by any means but that they could see we had certain things we wanted our children to be trained in.

Before we had our kids, people would tease and tell us to quickly write our book on parenting for when we had kids, we would change our mind about many things and not know "how to" parent anymore. I really believe it is important to talk and plan before we have children so that when they arrive there is a plan. Certainly, be

Deut. 5:16

flexible with that plan but have a plan! So, jokes aside, write your book, and make a plan now. I pray that all parents would be "intentional" in this way.

Our attitude and lifestyle will be our children's attitude and lifestyle. What they see they will do. Our actions speak so much louder than our words. They will learn their first lessons in Christianity from how we attempt to live for Christ. Strangely and very fortunately our children do not expect us to be perfect. They do however look for genuine effort and transparency in our walk.

I love what our brother Paul says to us in Ephesians 4:1-2 "I therefore, a prisoner for the Lord, urge you to walk in a manner worthy of the calling to which you have been called, with all humility and gentleness, with patience, bearing with one another in love."

Voice regularly the fact that you do not expect them to be what others expect them to be. That list would be different from person to person anyway and totally unreachable and unrealistic. Don't allow them to succumb to those pressures. Let them know that you are proud of their personal growth as Christians and never as "preacher's kids."

My parents did a marvelous job of affirming and encouraging us. They did challenge us to grow as Christians, but never did I feel that they wanted me to rise to a higher or different standard because I was a minister's or missionary's daughter. That was very freeing. Our children care what we think and expect much more than any outsider. Learning to filter out what others expect and focus only on what God expects of them is a life lesson we must teach our children. They can handle all kinds of peer and "other" pressure so long as they know we are not unrealistic and harsh in our expectations of them.

Help your children to prepare responses for those who lay this burden on them. They may need to think about polite, kind ways to say to people "As a Christian we are all expected to do such and such." Encourage them to pray for those who are immature and demanding in their expectations.

I recall we had trouble with a forty-year-old man in our congregation who picked on me and my mom. He expected things from me that a Christian of fifty years would have had trouble attaining never mind that I was a mere thirteen-year-old. He really did have the stereotype of "perfect preacher's kid." My mom and dad talked to us about trying to understand how he grew up, where he was in terms of spiritual growth, etc. This left a deep impression on my older brother and me. It modeled for us how to be merciful and able to give grace to someone who needed it. It taught us patience with others in their daily walk. They could have reacted in many negative ways and missed this chance to teach. My mom tells of finding my brother's prayer list in his bedroom while he was at school. She cried when she saw this man's name at the top of Stan's prayer list. Stan and I learned to pity and pray for those who struck out at us through this and many good uses of "teachable events."

Communication with our children is so important. I cannot emphasize enough how vital for your children this openness, this unconditional listening, is to building the lines of communication for the rest of their lives. Take time to answer all questions, to listen to those "tedious" stories. They need to know that in all the world you are the one most excited to hear what they have on their hearts.

In order to do this kind of listening, you and your husband will need to do some serious, intentional prioritizing. Talk with your husband about what is first in your family. Make the sacrifices that are needed to put you at home. Titus 2:4-5 tells young women to learn to "love their husbands and children, to be self-controlled, pure, working at home, kind, and submissive to their own husbands, that the word of God many not be reviled." We made the decision before we married that when children were given to us, I would be home. Whether you do this or not, home must be the focus of your life when you choose to have children. We felt that if I was home fulltime (even though I did some work from home where the kids could be with me), that we could better achieve our goal of bringing them up in the nurture and admonition of the Lord. I will talk more in a later chapter about some practical ways to be frugal, enabling families to do this.

One thing you will never regret doing in your life is spending time with your kids. Every funeral I have been to where the woman was beloved and lovely, the one thing said most often of her is the way she spent time raising her children. If there was one thing I could beg women to do it would be to stay home with your children. No one in the universe can replace mom. No nanny, no babysitter, no grandma, no daycare can ever touch what "mom" can do for her own precious children. It is worth every bit of sacrifice, every "thing" you will do without.

Be there to hold them, correct them, train them, listen to them, teach them daily God's word. All of this takes time and energy. Childhood does not last long, and we must use every minute to train and shape these little hearts. "You shall teach them diligently to your children and shall talk of them when you sit in your house, and when you walk by the way, and when you lie down, and when you rise. You shall bind them as a sign on your hand, and they shall be as frontlets between your eyes. You shall write them on the doorposts of your house and on your gates" (Deuteronomy 6:7-9).

My kids can tell you I took this verse quite literally. I did write or print many verses for us to memorize and stuck them everywhere in our house. I wanted to use every way I could to put the law on their hearts. Psalm 119:11 tells us "I have stored up your word in my heart, that I might not sin against you."

Being able to teach our children God's word will take time. Notice how every valuable, important thing we do takes that valuable commodity, time? We have to have time with them in large chunks where we can help them memorize, discuss and meditate on what God says.

Speaking of memorization, many young mothers ask me what their kids should know by certain ages. This really encourages me as it tells me that there are serious minded parents out there who pray and plan for their children's spiritual growth. We all know doctors have a checklist for where most kids should be in growth and development by certain ages. Shouldn't we make some sort of schedule or benchmark for this much more important type of growth?

Here are some of the goals we set for our three children as they were growing up in our home. Our children are 38, 36 and 32 so in some ways we are finished with their training. However, we still try to encourage them to keep growing and challenging themselves in the Lord. I hope this will not be seen as a legalistic list but rather as help to map out a plan for continual growth. Couple this with HUGE servings of humility and hours of prayer.

1-4 years
- Learn all the books of the Bible in order (Kids learn numbers and alphabet at this age, why not God's books?). Modify this goal according to a child's ability. Try it; you'll be amazed how quickly they catch on. Do it every day for two or three minutes when you have your family devotions.

25

- Teach parts of memory verses such as Eph. 6:1 "Children obey your parents in the Lord for this is right" or John 3:16, or Gen. 1:1.
- Using an accurate Bible storybook, start reading to them about every major Bible character. Some good ones are: *The Beginner's Bible*, *Egermeier's Bible Story Book* and *Hurlbut's Story of the Bible*. Show them in your Bible where these stories can be found. Tell them the Bible story is based on God's word. They need to see us upholding God's word all the time. Explain that these stories are different from fairy tales or make-believe stories that we read to them. Remember, repetition at this age is a way kids love to learn, so don't worry when they want the same story read over and over again. Read with expression, ask lots of questions, and review past stories. Use flannelgraph and good pictures. Have them draw pictures about the characters. Display these proudly so they learn that you value these stories.

5-8 years

- Learn the 12 sons of Jacob, the 12 apostles, the divisions of the Old and New Testament, Psalm 1, Psalm 23, and the sermon on the mount.
- Use Hurlbut's and Egermeier's now, they need more detail. Ask lots of questions.
- Make a simple timeline that you can roll up and store; add as you learn new events and people. Show the different dispensations: Patriarchal, Mosaic and Christian. Show them where they are on the timeline. They need to understand that they figure in God's overall plan. Have them look up the text for each story so that they begin to know how to find things in their own Bible.
- Make a game of finding passages quickly!
- Have them find the text of the sermon on Sundays. Challenge them to see how many times the speaker uses certain key words such as faith, grace, baptism, holy spirit, love and so on. All of this helps them see that they are part of the congregational worship period too.

9-12 years

- Learn selected passages as a family, like Philippians 2:1-11, or memorize certain Proverbs.

- This is the age where discussion of attitudes, motivations, etc. can be met with passages from the word. Show them how very practical and applicable the word is.
- We had our children complete some of the Bible correspondence courses that we offered at church. This is important as they grow toward the decision to become a Christian. Show them how to establish a daily time alone to read the Bible.
- We bought our children a one–year Bible, which has a reading for every day of the year. Each day has an Old Testament passage, a New Testament one and a Proverb and Psalm for the day. Even if they only read a small part of the daily allotment the habit of daily time with God will begin. Ask them periodically if they are doing it. Be gentle and encouraging, not harsh and demanding.
- We ask about school homework, how much more is there a need to ask about this more important area of their lives? Help them understand that you struggle with setting time aside and that failure one day does not mean that it is time to give up.

13 and up

- This is a time to study selected doctrinal subjects. Discuss areas that they are being challenged with or that they have questions about.
- We used the book of Proverbs extensively during this period. Help them see passages that deal with attitudes such as anger, lust, laziness, language, friends, entertainment, modesty…
- Read good articles, books and inspirational biographies with them.
- Subscribe to good Christian magazines and critically analyze articles together.
- Help them see that the walk with Christ is a growing one. Let them see you reading and challenging yourself. No child will do any of these things if they see their parents as fake or false.
- Talk to them about things you have struggled with and how you want to keep growing. Don't leave the impression that you have arrived.

- This is a really rich time for parents and teens or young adults. Be a listener; don't jump on them when they express doubts or questions.
- Be patient, answer lovingly, using "Let's see what the Bible says" every time. Never let them think we do things just through habit and tradition but because God says so in His word.

Another area all mothers need to work on is training our children to worship with the whole church. It is very good to have classes on our children's age level, but they also need to be taught to be a part of the whole church worshipping God. Too often we cheat them of the wonderful blessing of seeing all of us sing, pray, listen to the word, give and partake of the Lord's supper. We separate them out from the "adult" worship for one geared to them. Instead, we should sit with them in the pew and help them find the song in the book that the whole church is about to sing.

They need to learn to follow the lesson by turning to the passage and writing some words from the lesson. This will hopefully grow into "taking notes" as they get older. When our kids were too young to write I kept a "church bag" that had things in it they only got to see and touch during the lesson. I made sure there were only books, puzzles, and coloring books that were about God in that bag (I kept an eye open at the dollar store and other places for little things like this). They soon learned that we didn't read about Humpty Dumpty during church. This was early training in understanding what worship time IS about.

Our kids will take cues from us about how we act in worship. Are we excited to get to worship, like David who said, "I was glad when they said to me, 'Let us go to the house of the Lord'" (Psalm 122:1)? Do they see and hear how we anticipate with pleasure and joy our times of worship with our church? Do they watch how we spend Saturday night to ensure rest and readiness for our day of worship? Do we prepare our clothes for worship the night before so that Sunday morning is calm and not a time of frantically looking for shoes, socks, clothes, etc.? Plan ahead.

It is amazing to me how children can learn to do anything we decide to teach them. They can learn to sit quietly. They can learn to use the bathroom before worship, so they do not need to walk out during the service. They can learn to imitate what they see adults do. We don't challenge them enough in this area.

Several places we have been we have challenged all the kids in the church family to take notes. My brother, Stan Mitchell, made a nice "Eutychus and You" page that can be found at the end of this book. One side is for note taking and one for drawing something from the lesson. He rewarded the kids at his congregation with a stick of gum if they did this. Similarly, I gave our congregation's kids Laffy Taffy or some candy. It was fun to see how their note taking grew and how the pictures drawn were truly reflective of the lesson. It taught them they really were able to be a part of the worship period by teaching them they could understand and learn from what was preached.

Our religion is a practical one. Work in the kingdom with your children right next to you. They must see all of this good teaching has a practical application. Open your home for hospitality, Bible studies, and devotions. Let them know that God gave you your home and talents for His kingdom. Bake muffins and take them to the discouraged, the elderly, the visitor. Take them to clean someone's home or do yard work. Doing these acts of kindness with them will have a greater impact than any words you can speak. The words are important, but the actions are what convinces them that you are sincere. Show them that you want to be the hands and feet of Jesus.

As a child I spent many hours visiting the hospital and visiting people's homes with either my dad or mom. They took me with them joyfully. I never had the feeling that they were doing these things under compulsion or duress. We thought it was fun.

I remember seeing this joyful visitation in another sweet family several years ago when my mom lay dying in KU Medical Center in Kansas City. The Roger Chaffin family were working with the Raytown church of Christ and would come to visit mom and me in the hospital. Their youngest Naomi was probably about three. They brought her with them. She sang "Jesus loves me" for my mom. Mom was not able to talk much anymore but I remember how brightly her eyes shone and how big she smiled to see and hear this little visitor learning to "minister" to others alongside her parents. What a gift they had given Naomi in training her to have compassion and love for those in pain. Don't hesitate to take your children and serve others. The reward is eternal.

God put wonderful heroes in His word for us to emulate. Try to think of some who inspire you to be a better parent, such as Mary –

who pondered things in her heart: "But Mary treasured up all these things, pondering them in her heart" (Luke 2:19). We need to be very thoughtful about the way we parent. There is no more important job on earth than to lead these souls to heaven. I would love to have seen how Mary and Joseph parented. God knew He had to choose the best mom for His own son.

What kind of time and effort did she put into raising the son of God? She was not perfect. In fact, she could be pushy: "the mother of Jesus said to him 'They have no wine.' And Jesus said to her 'Woman what does that have to do with me? My hour has not yet come.'" (John 2:3-4). Then He immediately performed His first miracle. He also loved her so much that as He hung on the cross in excruciating pain, He thought to make sure she would be cared for when He was gone. "When Jesus saw his mother and the disciple whom he loved standing nearby, he said to his mother, 'Woman, behold your son!' Then he said to the disciple, 'Behold, your mother'" (John 19:26, 27). She inspired great caring and love. She had been the kind of thoughtful mother we should take the time to aspire to be.

We can never pray enough for our children and for ourselves as parents. Hannah is my ideal praying and teaching mom. She prayed so hard that the priest Eli thought she was drunk. She told Eli "No, my lord, I am a woman troubled in spirit. I have drunk neither wine nor strong drink, but I have been pouring out my soul before the Lord." (I Samuel 1:15). Do we pour out our souls to God concerning our children?

Hannah must have spent much time teaching Samuel so that he would be ready to leave his mama and go work in the tabernacle. She was also a very grateful mom and one willing to see that her child was not hers forever. "I have lent him to the Lord. As long as he lives, he is lent to the Lord" (1 Samuel 1:28). Our children are not ours forever: have we prayed and taught them well enough that we can release them at such a young age as Samuel was?

Every morning I pray for our children and try to do as Job did with regard to his children. "And when the days of the feast had run their course, Job would send and consecrate them, and he would rise early in the morning and offer burnt offerings according to the number of them all. For Job said, 'It may be that my children have sinned and cursed God in their hearts.' Thus Job did continually" (Job 1:5). Job was not just concerned for outwardly obvious sins but sins his children might have committed in their hearts. We need to be in prayer daily for the inner persons of our children. We need to be on our knees asking God to help them grow in faith and in purity.

One of the most important things my parents did for us and that we tried our best to do with our family was to have daily family devotions. Here is an article my mom wrote in the 1990s about how they did this.

Family Devotions

"And these words that I command you today shall be on your heart. You shall teach them diligently to your children and shall talk of them when you sit in your house, and when you walk by the way and when you lie down, and when you rise. You shall bind them as a sign on your hand, and they shall be as frontlets between your eyes." Deuteronomy 6:6-8

"Fathers do not provoke your children to anger but bring them up in the discipline and instruction of the Lord." Ephesians 6:4

God gave His people the awesome responsibility of training their children in the right way. This task cannot be done by a Bible class teacher who spends less than two hours each week with your children. It must be a daily habit with planned devotionals and making use of every teachable moment that may arise during the course of the day.

Babies love songs and simple Bible story illustrations. Christian mothers, take time to teach your little ones; do not leave it to someone else.

Loy and I began to have devotionals together before we were married and have continued throughout our marriage. It was not always easy while the children were growing up, but we managed to have a set time each day to sit down for ten to twenty minutes to read the Bible, pray and sing. When the children were small, we read simple Bible stories to them. Egermeier's and Hurburt's were used as well as various Ladybird books and Golden books. We read Mrs. Lee's Stories About Jesus and found that the children loved to answer the questions given at the end of each story. *The Beginner's Bible* by Karyn Henley has been read and enjoyed by our grandchildren.

We also drilled the children on memory verses, books of the Bible, sons of Jacob, apostles, etc. This was sometimes done as we travelled to shop. Friday afternoons we had neighborhood classes in which we sang, read stories, used visual aids to illustrate stories, dramatized Bible events or watched Bible film strips. For several years Loy managed to be at home for devotional around four in the afternoon and the neighborhood playmates happily joined the family. If you have guests, do not skip family worship; invite your guests to join you or to sit comfortably while you spend a few minutes at the "family altar."

As time went on and the children had school activities in the afternoons, we had our Bible reading at the breakfast table and this has continued to today, though the children are gone. We have read through special articles and lectureship books, used different Bible versions and read application stories and books like *Must The Young Die Too?*

Our children loved to have someone read to them because we read appropriate children's stories to them at an early age, often before an afternoon rest. If you have not established the reading habit early, they may be restless about sitting for devotional. Make the time short and use songs and stories suitable to their age levels.

Some time ago a church bulletin listed suggestions for family devotions. Following are some of them in brief.

1. Be enthusiastic.
2. Plan ahead.
3. Make lessons encouraging to the children.
4. Choose a consistent time.
5. Make sure all the family is present.
6. Involve older children in leading prayers, songs etc.
7. Teach children how to sit, sing, pray and be like Jesus.
8. Use visual aids.
9. Teach concepts repeatedly.
10. Try new settings – sunrise, sunset, campfire, the park and other places.

Do not underestimate the impact made on children by having regular devotionals. Not long ago we met a man who had boarded with us for a term while he was in high school and could not get a place in the school hostel. He told us he remembered and appreciated our family worship and said he would like to train his children in like manner. We had often felt that this adolescent boy was bored and sometimes rebellious about our "spiritual habits."

God bless you and your family. You have a fearful and wonderful privilege.

Donna Mitchell, Mutare, Zimbabwe

We are people of faith because of someone in our lives before us. Whether they are biological family or others who become our parents and grandparents in the faith, we owe a debt to those who taught us. Paul says to Timothy "I am reminded of your sincere faith, a faith that dwelt first in your grandmother Lois and your mother Eunice and now, I am sure, dwells in you as well" (2 Timothy 1:5). Again, He says, "From childhood you have been acquainted with the sacred writings, which are able to make you wise for salvation through faith in Christ Jesus" (2 Timothy 3:15). Have we taught our children as well as Lois and Eunice did? Will it be said confidently of our children that this faith "I am sure dwells in you as well" as Paul did when speaking to young Timothy?

We need to see the people in the Bible as very real and very necessary as examples to us as mothers. Lois was the mother of a young preacher. She did not know what he would do later as a young man. She just knew he needed knowledge of God's holy word. So, she and her mom taught him well and then when he followed God's leading into ministry, he was equipped for it.

Grandparents are so important to the raising of a new generation of the faithful. I discovered this verse while creating some lessons for a ladies' day in Kansas. My topic was "Blessed is the nation." This verse tells us how we can build a multi-generational heritage of faith: "Only take care, and keep your soul diligently, lest you forget the things that your eyes have seen, and lest they depart from your heart all the days of your life. Make them known to your children and your children's children" (Deuteronomy 4:9).

What a great challenge was given to Israel. In order for the next generation to remain faithful, parents AND grandparents must first live God's way themselves and then teach them to their children and grandchildren. We as grandparents need to find ways to be in our grandkids' lives as spiritual guides. Forget the toys and cute clothes, instead imprint them with the faith that you treasure.

My dad was one of ten children raised on a Kansas farm in the middle of the 1900's. My grandmother Maude did not know as she taught those ten children and lived a joyful example of Christian life that the seven sons God gave her would all be preachers. Three went to the foreign mission field. She had no way of knowing that God had these plans for her children. She just knew they needed to know what God wanted them to live like as His people. We need to teach our children every minute we can while we have them so that we too

33

can "lend them to the Lord" as Hannah did.

When our children see our joy in serving God, they will be able to handle the pressure that is often put on them in their position. Their souls are more important to you than any soul in the world. My dad always said if he won a million souls to the Lord and lost one of the four of us, he would feel he failed.

We knew that was how he felt. We heard him say it but more importantly we knew it by the way he really did put us first. He made sure that Friday nights and Saturdays were our family days. He did not schedule studies for those times. We did things as a family. Saturdays, mom would cook hot dogs or hamburgers or make sandwiches, and we drove up into the mountains surrounding Mutare, Zimbabwe, where we were missionaries. We hiked, played ball and ate out in God's gorgeous creation. We usually had three or four extra kids, as mom and dad encouraged us to invite friends to the house or on outings. This "fun" time was added to the daily family devotions that we had from the time we were tiny until we left for college. Dad had daily devotions with his second wife Debbie, up till the day he gained his reward. When we visited them, it was like slipping back into the past as we sang, prayed and read together. As a family, we all treasure the memory of hearing his morning reading. Make certain you are building those habits in your children and they will have the tools to withstand any criticism.

This task of training and teaching these precious souls is so very important. Perhaps you can use this prayer to help: *Dear Lord, When you called me to be a mama, you didn't ask for perfection but that with every breath I'd point them to you.*

Questions

1. What does it mean to be intentional as parents?
2. What is the most important thing we need to teach our children according to Ephesians 6:1 and Proverbs 22:6?
3. Is loving our husband and children an easy and "natural" thing? Read Titus 2:4-5. Who can help us learn to love our children better?
4. Ask older women, whom you admire for raising their children, how they created a daily devotion or Bible time with their kids. Pick their brains and use ideas that seem suited to your family.
5. Look at your planner or calendar and delete things that are not helping your family grow closer to God. Remember James 4:8 "Draw near to God, and he will draw near to you."

Chapter 5: The Empty Nest Years

God gives us seasons of life. Ecclesiastes 3:1 says, "For everything there is a season, and a time for every matter under heaven." I need to keep that passage in mind every day. An awareness that God gives us a variety of experiences and that He expects us to live these experiences fully. Accepting His timing, His plan for each season in our lives is so important in becoming that "intentional" woman. We need to stop living in either the past or the future. Live in the time God has given us now. The empty nest years are one of those wonderful "seasons" that God gives us.

I loved raising my children, but the empty nest years are wonderful too. I have more time to teach women and children. I can travel and be with my husband as he makes calls and studies with people. I do not have the responsibilities of childcare and in my case of homeschooling that I had when the kids were home. This "freedom" came along gradually as our children left home one at a time. This is yet another season of life that God gives us and expects us to use wisely as women and as ministry people. We have many unique opportunities.

There are certain blessings and responsibilities that come along with this season of empty nesters. The rest of the chapter is devoted to those.

Know Self

By this age we have perhaps had twenty or more years of experience in marriage, raising children and in getting along with people. We have had time to experience some good things and some difficult things. This means we have something to share from our own bumps and bruises. When we share our personal experience and trials, our teaching is much richer and stronger. We have an authenticity that we could not have had when we were young and untried.

With age comes a knowledge of self that enables us to work smarter. We don't waste time experimenting anymore because we know what we are good at and what we are not. We have learned skills in other areas that we can utilize for the Lord. We are not as shy to step out and volunteer and lead. Being competent and capable in other areas of life gives us confidence and with good reason. We are wiser now than when we were young and still having to learn skills.

This should prepare us for leadership. We have skills and wisdom and the time now to use both. God has put us in this spot for the good of the kingdom. We should not fight God's leading and provision of opportunities. This is a time to look for and ask for areas to lead and serve in. We must not be like the one talent man who hid his talent. Instead, we should be like the multi-talent man who received more when he used what he was given (Matthew 25:14-30).

Example Teaches

Whether we are in full time church work or not, as older women we are commanded to share with others our wisdom and experience. Titus 2:3-5 says "Older women likewise are to be reverent in behavior, not slanderers or slaves to much wine. They are to teach what is good, and so train the young women to love their husbands and children, to be self-controlled, pure, working at home, kind, and submissive to their own husbands, that the word of God may not be reviled." We are to set an example by our holy, reverent living. We are not to be addicted to anything: alcohol, drugs, prescription or otherwise.

We are to be teaching what is good. So, what is good? Teaching the young women to love their husbands and children. This loving does not come naturally. Anything we have to learn is not instinctive; it has to be taught. Teaching involves words and actions. Our example as wives and moms will illustrate what this love looks like

This powerful thing called example is so vital in the area of marriage. Are we examples of respect for our husbands? Ephesians 5:33 says "let the wife see that she respects her husband" and I Peter 3:1-6 talks about how our submission to our husbands will be what wins even an unbelieving husband over. No words should be necessary. Our actions should show him how we honor him. We need to be like Sarah who obeyed Abraham and even showed that respect by calling him master. She was a beautiful woman because her life was pure, gentle and submissive. Submission is a very difficult thing for human beings. And like many hard to achieve things, when it is seen, it is truly beautiful.

a wife needs to be ADORED
a husband needs to be ADMIRED.

We do not like the idea of submission. Our culture tells us that submission is weakness. Our culture tells us that we have "our rights." But God's own son was willing to give up His "rights" so we could be saved. Jesus honored the Father by being submissive. Philippians 2:6-8 says several things about His attitude. He "did not count equality with God something to be grasped, but made himself nothing, taking the form of a servant... He humbled himself by becoming obedient to the point of death— even death on a cross." He respected His father. What a beautiful relationship we see between Jesus and His father. We older women need to respect and honor our husbands like Jesus respected and honored His father. How very powerful that example will be!

As a preacher's wife, the younger women will look to me even more than other older women in the body of Christ. There is no way to change this. I need to trust that God will enable me to live like He tells me to so that I can be a light. Am I living in a way that sets an example in my marriage for the younger women who I hope to teach? Do they see me speak kindly, politely, and lovingly to my husband or do they hear me being curt and sharp with him? Do they hear me praise him when he is not around or do they hear me carp and gripe about what he does or doesn't do? Our words and attitudes teach so much. They reveal what we truly believe.

Many times, when a group of women gets together for coffee, the conversation descends into a husband bashing session. Wouldn't it be wonderful if, instead, our younger women only ever heard us praising and honoring our husbands? What powerful teaching that would be! By the way, this applies to how we speak about our children too. Do we whine about things our children are doing when we are together? Do we put them down and talk as if they are a burden instead of the very great gift God has given us? God says "Like arrows in the hand of a warrior are the children of one's youth. Blessed is the man who fills his quiver with them" (Psalm 127:4-5a).

I Thessalonians 5:18 tells us "Give thanks in all circumstances." What would our life be like if we found something to thank God for in every situation? Pollyanna's "glad game" actually displays a godly attitude, one of optimism based on thanks. If we found things to be thankful about in our husbands and children every day, we would have an easier time learning to love them.

Do these younger women see me unhesitatingly serve my husband or am I waiting for him to take "his turn" at serving? Jesus did not hesitate to serve. He did not wait for the apostles to take their turn before He washed their feet. There is a kind of "clout" that will come with our teaching if we are living or attempting to live what our words say.

When I began thinking of writing this book, I asked for opinions, questions, advice and ideas from preacher's wives of all ages. I loved reading what I got back, but one thing I really enjoyed was the wisdom given to me from women in this stage of life. It was tested wisdom. We finally have a store of experiences that give us freedom to advise. I will try to share some of the advice from these older women. God obviously thinks we have something to share since He commands ALL older women to teach the younger ones.

By our forties and fifties, we have had time to really know what our strengths and weaknesses are. We now know our limitations and strengths This helps us not waste time since we know what we are capable of. We can step out and use that confidence in the kingdom.

Age and experience help us to be more tactful. Tact and manners go a long way to easing problems or preventing difficulties. We have had enough experience that we can anticipate the train wreck before it happens. We know what will ignite problems with the women and can advise the group about how to avoid that. When I was young, I did not always consider the whole group and the various ages and needs of our women. The longer I live, the more I see that we need much more time with all ages to help us all learn from one another.

Last year I had the privilege to speak at a ladies' retreat in Tennessee. Our youngest woman was 21 and our oldest 88 with forty-five women ranging in age between those two. What a blessing, as we had our discussions, to hear what the needs and opinions were of the very young and the wisdom of the older women. Why should our young women and middle aged for that matter have to make the same mistakes the older made when the older can warn and help them by telling their stories or listening quietly to the young and then helping them see some different solutions?

Our goal should be to be like that worthy woman in Proverbs 31:26 – "She opens her mouth with wisdom, and the teaching of kindness is on her tongue." I am certain from the description of her household that the worthy woman was not in her twenties. She had life experience in business, marriage and child raising. Her children were able to appreciate their mom and therefore were able to "rise up and call her blessed" (Proverbs 31:28a).

Be Available

Since we do not have the responsibilities of children in this stage, we have the time to be available. We have more time to make visits and to go to events where our members and children of the church are participating. I am always amazed how going to a school play, recital, concert or sports event will win the hearts of the child as well as the child's parent. This is such a simple and seemingly small thing, yet our presence tells them that we care and are interested in what they do.

This is a time when we can invite people over more. We don't have as many mouths to feed all week so we should have more time and money to be hospitable. I will talk more about how to be hospitable later, but this is a reminder that we can do simple things and invite people into our wonderful homes. Look around and find the young women who do not have family and invite them for Sunday lunch. Use your memory and recall how much not having to make a meal on Sunday or a weeknight would have lightened your load when you were a young woman. Again, this puts us with the younger families who need our encouragement and help.

When we are in our homes, we are more ourselves, and young families can observe our interactions with our husbands and can watch us as we practice love and hospitality. We cannot do the teaching and encouraging that we need to by only interacting with people at church services. We need to be with each other in everyday situations.

The very best things in life are free. Our best gift to others is our time. In monetary terms it costs us nothing. Yet it is the best thing we can give. We need to take time to talk to teens in our churches and listen to them. How hard is that? They are living in a tough, wicked world. They need to know we are in their corner, that we are praying for them, that we love them and that we want them to be powerful people in the kingdom. These empty nest years we have more time we can invest in them.

One dear friend of ours who grew up as the only Christian in his family directly relates his remaining faithful to some elders in his church who took time to show interest in him. They took time to speak to him on the street, away from the meetings as well as at church. They invited him into their homes. They urged him to go to a Christian college where he learned more about how to create a Christian home and that was where he found his wife. It is such a very simple thing to show interest in someone. It took that free thing: time.

Many of my friends are in this stage of their lives and they are developing or pursuing hobbies they didn't have time for when they were younger. We could make "others" our hobby. Or we could include others in our hobbies as a way to have time with them. What are your gifts? How can you use those gifts now that you have more time to help the kingdom grow?

As I have sat writing this book, I have longed to pick up the phone and talk to my mom asking for her input. She has gone on to our Lord, but I am blessed by the many things she wrote. I have her lesson plans in a filing cabinet that I treasure. She wrote the article following this paragraph. She and I really enjoyed our partnership in the kingdom. We often taught classes together. Our teaching styles complemented each other. Once again, I am able to share her work in this book.

The Empty Nest by Donna Mitchell

Solomon wrote in Ecclesiastes 3 that there is a season for everything. Our nests empty earlier than our grandmothers' did and we can use this time in greater service to God. Possibly, we feel that we are no longer needed, and we are made aware of the brevity of life (James 4:14). But what a joyful time this can be!

Have you prepared for the empty nest? If we have had a good marriage relationship, it should now be enriched. Genesis 2:24 teaches that the married couple is to leave parents and cleave to one another. We did that before our children came - have we preserved the closeness of our earlier relationship? Ephesians 5:21-33 describes a very close relationship between husband and wife. My husband should remain my priority before my children; I must find time to nourish our bond of communication. Abraham and Sarah continued to love one another throughout their lives; Aquila and Priscilla worked together in teaching the gospel to others.

We must prepare to release our children. Returning to Genesis 2:24 we are reminded that they, too, must leave father and mother. We should have taught them daily (Deuteronomy 6:1-9), preparing them for life. We should have lived the dedicated life of a disciple for them to see. We should have honored our own parents and taught them the necessity of honoring theirs.

Having sent them into their new lives, what must we do now?

We can reassess our goals and purposes in life. Reflect on past losses, good times, gains, new relationships and old relationships. Help our children to achieve oneness in their families (Ephesians 5:31) and to lovingly accept their spouses' families, but support them from a distance, not as an authority.

Evaluate our lives. Where have we been? Where are we going? What do we want from life now?

It is a time of decision. There is great potential in the older person or couple. They can spend quality time with their spouses, their friends and their aged parents. They can do the Lord's work, using their experience and maturity in teaching and leading others to Christ. There is a group of retired people in the Unites States who travel around the country in caravans, stopping to spend several weeks with churches that can use their help in Holiday Bible schools and other programs of work. Some retired people have gone to other countries to preach and teach.

Indeed, there is a time for everything, and this can be a time for thanksgiving, of seeing goals fulfilled and accepting the fact that some weren't fulfilled. Think of the good that Paul did in his midlife years.

Anxiously anticipate the future; do not waste time brooding over the past. We have found our empty nest, which often is not empty, the best time yet!

Donna Mitchell, Mutare Zimbabwe

My mom wrote that short article for a southern African audience in their empty nest years. They had returned to Zimbabwe where they had worked while we children were growing up. They labored there that second time twelve years. They were able to do different things without the need to consider raising kids. They also had the wisdom that only age, and experience can give. They were enriched workers in the kingdom. Imagine how much richer your ministry will be with your husband after you have been a team for twenty or thirty years. After all, they are not empty years, just an empty nest.

Questions

1. What does Ecclesiastes 3:1 mean? How does that apply to you?
2. Make a list of older women in the Bible who were in this empty nest stage of life. Describe what their attitude was.
3. What does Matthew 25:14-30 teach about using what God has given us?

Chapter 6: Wife on the Mission Field

My parents Loy and Donna Mitchell left the USA March 16, 1958 for Nhowe Mission in Southern Rhodesia (now Zimbabwe). They were 26 and 25, had one child, Stanley age 18 months, and had never been outside the States until then. I am filled with admiration for such nerve, faith and dedication. They went from a first world lifestyle with running water, electricity, smooth roads, well stocked stores and lots of family, to a place that did not have any of those things. Plus, they would have to learn a totally new culture. They had to become like babies in this host country, learning like all babies do, by imitation, repetition and trial and error.

A missionary's wife has a whole different set of expectations and obligations than most ministry wives have. She not only is a minister's wife and has the pressures and duties that go with that role, but she often has to do it "blind" in a sense. She will have to learn to do ministry in a new culture. As a preacher's wife in the culture we grew up in, we at least know the culture, the church and the society. It is our home culture. A missionary and his wife are taking a crash course in the culture and society of their adopted country.

I grew up admiring and making missionary wives my faith heroes. The best way I know to help you see how a wife on the mission field lives is to describe some of the ones I was blessed to observe. I got to see clearly at an early age how many different ways ministry can be done. I saw how many different personality types there can be in the church and how that actually makes the church stronger and better. I saw missionaries on a mission station working together and then I got to watch missionaries in an urban setting become a team. It's tragic when we, as a church, think all workers should be the same and approach things in the same way, when in fact the many body parts concept is so much healthier.

As I was preparing for this book, I found again some treasures my mom had written. Since she died, anything she wrote seems twice as precious to me and my siblings. Here is an article my mom wrote after one of her faith heroes, another missionary wife, passed on to her reward. Mom felt, as I do, that we owe such a debt to older missionaries who set wonderful examples of faith for us.

A Worthy Woman

"......teach the older women to be reverent in the way they live...then they can train the younger women..." (Titus 2:3-4).

I am only one of many women who were influenced by Nancy A'Delia Short. She died recently in Cordell, Oklahoma. Her daughter, Beth Ewing, observed that it was as though she was making a journey for which she had prepared many years. I first met "Mother" Short in 1958 while we lived at Nhowe mission in Southern Rhodesia (now Zimbabwe). I was expecting our second child when we traveled to Bulawayo for a gospel meeting and the Shorts were visiting from Namwianga Mission. (Our baby, another Nancy, was born a month later and is now a missionary wife and mother in Zimbabwe). Mother Short gathered me into her arms and heart and called me one of her daughters. I was young and homesick in a strange land, but I had found a mother in Africa!

Later, at Nhowe Mission, I remember watching her as she opened her Bible to Proverbs 31 and taught the African women. She exemplified the worthy woman, and my thoughts recalled her early days in Africa. She and Daddy Short arrived in Southern Rhodesia in 1921 with their baby son. They moved on to Sinde Mission in Northern Rhodesia where they lived in a two-room pole and mud hut with no doors and windows while they made bricks and built a more substantial house. In those days the wild animals roamed the country freely; they could imagine a lion walking through that open door! Transportation meant walking eight miles to a railway siding, riding a bicycle or using an ox drawn sledge. Sister Short was on the mission eight months before she left the place. When she did leave, it was in answer to a message that her husband, away preaching in a village, had become very ill. She walked to the railway siding and discovered that the train would not arrive until the next day.

Margaret and Foy Short told this story about the Shorts. "Mother was on a village trip with Daddy when Brother Lawyer was killed. They had taken Beth with them and left Foy and Sybil behind. They had gone on a train to Kashitu siding and then hired a man with a lorry to take them 35 miles into the bush, arranging with him to come back later to take them back to the siding. Runners came with the message about Brother Lawyer, that he had been seriously injured, so they started walking back. They sent a runner back to ask the lorry to come for them, but they had walked 30 miles when the lorry came for them. They started walking at 9:00 at night, walked until 2:00, rested until 3:00, then walked on. Some boys were carrying Beth in a machila (like a stretcher or hammock). When they got back to Senkoba they had to walk the 8 miles to the mission because no one knew when they were coming."

We felt the influence of these devoted Christians everywhere we worked. Many years later as we preached in Umtali and the Eastern Highlands area, we met people who recalled the Bible studies taught by the Shorts while they lived on a farm. (Farming became a necessity for their livelihood in the 1935-1945 period when they did not receive enough support.)

Staying in the Short home was a wonderful blessing. As we prepared meals together, Mother Short and I talked of cooking, sewing, children and husbands in the Biblical context. Loy and Daddy Short spoke of the Lord's work as they prepared printed tracts and "Rays of Light" (a paper published by the Shorts for many years and used extensively in our work). They also knew how to relax and enjoy a break in routine. One time after a gospel meeting in Bulawayo, where they "retired to work some more," we said, "Come to Wankie Game Reserve with us!" They replied, "We'd like that!" and we set off. I shall always remember that trip as we viewed God's magnificent creatures in the wild, camped at night and worshipped together each morning and evening. I also recall that we stopped to encourage a family who had moved to Dett, an isolated place where no church met.

Sister Short's health failed a few years ago, and she was bedfast. It was her husband's custom to sit near her and read his Bible in the mornings while waiting for her to awaken. It was on such a morning in July of 1980, that he died quietly. Later their children brought their mother back to Cordell, Oklahoma. I could never imagine the two of them separated-now they are together once more.

Donna Mitchell

The first thing I would say to a missionary's wife is to make the decision to go to the mission field a mutual one. If you do not want to go to another country, let your husband know before you decide to go. It is not fair to keep your feelings and fears hidden from him in the mistaken notion that you have to go overseas or that you will overcome your fears. You may overcome them but not without admitting and sharing them with your best friend and partner.

This and ministry at home has to be something you both are ready for. You may have fears and reservations, but if you are willing, put those in God's hands, then venture forward enthusiastically and don't turn back. When talking to those who said they wanted to follow Him on this earth Jesus reminded them to count the cost of following Him. Then He said, "No one who puts his hand to the plow and looks back is fit for the kingdom of God" (Luke 9:62). Make the decision whether to serve here or abroad and then wherever you choose to serve, make that choice a good one by doing your best to stay on course.

Prepare well for the field. Today there are so many ways to prepare for missions. There are Bible schools, Christian colleges, and special facilities to prepare you for a cross cultural situation. Take the time to prepare. Don't rush in unprepared. Study the language and country you are going to. Speak to those with experience of the region. There is no way you will do away with culture shock. Homesickness is inevitable. But knowing a little of what to expect will go a long way to keep you on the road.

My mom often said the early missionaries of the twentieth century were better prepared for third world conditions as most of them had grown up on farms or as poorer people themselves. Most of our young adults considering the mission field today have grown up in middle class homes in the US where they have never had to do without, or had to deal with bureaucracy where there is no recourse. Thus, missions education is even more vital to help them deal with whatever their chosen host country's difficulties might be.

Be a part of the fund-raising process in whatever way you are gifted. Being by your husband's side when visiting churches that will be involved or possibly involved in your work will bond you as a couple and endear you to your future supporters. Supporting churches need to know you and bond with you. They will be more likely to pray for and financially care for a family who they have gotten to know as real individuals. You want to be able to say as Paul did "I thank my God in all my remembrance of you, always in every prayer of mine for you all making my prayer with joy, because of your partnership in the gospel from the first day until now" (Philippians 1:3-5). Missionaries cannot go without the senders. Spend time getting to know your partners in this important work.

We women have such great power in our homes to set the tone. If we whine and complain, if we see only difficulties and hardships, our family will too. Philippians 2:14-15 was a passage we tried to memorize and obey in our home: "Do all things without grumbling or disputing that you may be blameless and innocent, children of God without blemish in the midst of a crooked and twisted generation, among whom you shine as lights in the world." The missionary wives I admire are the ones who used this attitude in the challenges of preparing and going to the field.

Once she is on the field the missionary wife again must prioritize as any wife should: Husband and family first. Do not neglect your husband and children while trying to "save souls" in a foreign land. Your family's souls are your first responsibility. If you no longer have children to raise, then again you have more time but if you have children in the home, they must be your first priority. They need you. Take time to schedule your weeks so that you will not unwittingly slip into relegating family to last. It does not matter if others don't understand your priorities. Explain your philosophy and then do what is right.

I saw so many missionary families balance this. My dad often took care of us while mom went to teach the women in the villages or in the townships. Mom and Dad were partners in the word and partners in raising us.

Jim and Kay Petty were co-workers of my parents in Zimbabwe and later they worked in South Africa. When Bobby and I visited them in Empangeni, South Africa, we observed a very wise thing that they did. Jim would come home for an afternoon and watch their four kids every week so that Kay could go do anything she wanted to. This rest and recreation was so vital to her being able to be the good wife, mom and wonderful teacher she was. That was not achieved without a plan.

A theme I have heard as I have talked to missionary families from all over the world is the need to recharge. Encouragement is so necessary for the longevity of a work and of a couple's ministry wherever they might live. Many teams planned days where they took time off and "played" as a group. Times where they went hiking, camping, picnicked, sang and prayed as a group. The "Sabbath" principle of the Old Testament was so important for God's people then and we can learn a lot about rest and recharging from what God knew His people needed then. Even Jesus took time to be by Himself to gain strength. He prayed and spent time away from the crowds and He spent time in social activities that recharged Him like weddings and time with friends like Mary, Martha and Lazarus. We need to make sure we take time for these outlets too.

Some of my fondest memories are of missionary retreats we went to as a family while I was growing up. I got to meet and watch so many missionaries in the region we worked. Seeing godly men and women discuss scripture, their work, their struggles, laugh, sing, pray and play left an indelible mark on my faith. We often hosted fellow missionaries in our home and gave up our bedrooms so they could come stay with us for a rest or to take part in a meeting of some sort. What a great blessing we had to sit at the feet of these spiritual, but very real people.

If you and your husband plan to go to the mission field, please do not cut yourself off from other workers. Just as Hebrews 10:24 tells the church to meet together to "stir up one another to love and good works," missionaries need to make a plan to spend time together to keep each other strong for the work.

Informing your supporters is so very important. We have seen missionaries lose support just because they didn't take the time to write about what they were doing on the field. Help your husband do this. Or be the one who does this if that is part of your gift set. We are so blessed by technology today. Not only can we write a report and send it in seconds to our partners, but we have Facebook, skype, video and phone calls to keep us connected.

Don't be longwinded. Keep reports short and interesting. Make sure you make it personal. They want to know about their new brethren, but they most want to know what you are doing and what life is like for you. Schedule a time to do this every month. Take turns with your husband doing this or both of you have a part each month. Keep each other accountable in this.

One of the best tools on the mission field is hospitality. People who have been introduced to Jesus need to see how His people live. Open homes allow this. I will talk more about hospitality in another chapter but know that it is a great way to evangelize and later to ground the new church in how a Christian family should be. Not that the missionary family is perfect, but that it is often the only example of Christian family the new converts might see.

The home I grew up in was as busy as Grand Central station. My parents wanted us to feel free to bring home friends and we did in large numbers. Mom never complained; she said she would rather have our friends at our house than somewhere else where she and dad would not have input and control of the situation. But mom and dad always invited people over too. I am sure this was in large part due to the very good examples of hospitality mom and dad had seen in their homes growing up in Kansas and Oklahoma. Both the Taylors (mom's family) and the Mitchells (dad's family) were well known for an open door.

I would say all of the missionary families I knew were hospitable in this way and the church grew fast and strong because of it. Maybe that's why God tells us to be hospitable. "Do not neglect to show hospitality to strangers, for thereby some have entertained angels unawares" (Hebrews 13:2). I Peter 4:9 says, "Show hospitality to one another without grumbling." How very important to be open this way and how easy and cost effective. We need to open our homes and show others how Jesus lives in us and changes us.

Our "adopted" sister Jean Lambert who spent much time in our home in Zimbabwe growing up, watched and participated in our home's hospitality and when she built her own home, she emulated what she and her husband Don had seen in our home. Don had also seen and experienced such an example of hospitality because of the time he spent as a teen with other church workers, the Hatfields, in Bulawayo, Zimbabwe.

This good example continues in our homes and our children's homes. Hospitality is contagious. Just invite people in and treat them not as some guest you spend a week preparing for but as family. If it's cornbread and beans or a baloney sandwich, make others feel at home.

I pray that if you choose to be a missionary with your husband that you will lean on those who have been there before and humble yourself enough to learn from their wisdom and mistakes. God is the one who enables us all. Remember what Paul the missionary said, "I can do all things through him who strengthens me" (Philippians 4:13).

Questions

1. Should a wife be involved in the decision to go to the mission field?
2. How important is the "Sabbath" principle to a missionary?
3. Is hospitality necessary on the mission field?
4. Think of ways to encourage the next generation to dream of being missionaries.
5. Is reporting to supporters important? Why?

1 Tim. 5.10

Rom 12.13

Chapter 7: Why Hospitality?

During a Wednesday night summer series, we heard stories of coming to faith from some men in our congregation. One of my favorites had to do with hospitality. The young man said his dad began to "church hunt" when he was a young teen. One week they attended a church of Christ. A family in that church always prepared enough food every Sunday lunch for themselves and whoever was visiting. This family invited his family. They opened their home to total strangers every week. The young man's father was so impressed with this hospitality that he agreed to study with someone in the church and the whole household was saved. The dad didn't need to hear the doctrine taught to know that God was living in these people. The family sharing the hospitality weren't even the ones to do the actual Bible study, but their actions were what drew the family toward God. It is such a simple thing to open your home, and yet we do not do it as often as we should. Some of us do not practice hospitality at all. Maybe some of the practical ideas I have gleaned from my mom, my own experience and from some others who have given me advice will help us all to do better.

The smell of coffee, pot roast, hot rolls, pie fresh out of the oven, the cranking of the ice cream maker or the smell of homemade pancakes and syrup are smells synonymous with hospitality to me. They seem to reach out and welcome anyone. Sharing food, sharing conversation, sharing time. Sharing. We have almost lost the art of hospitality. Opening our homes and therefore our hearts to others is so very important. As Christians we need to relearn this grace. Hospitality is one of the most intimate types of giving. It requires opening up and being vulnerable enough to let people see who you really are.

Have you ever noticed that every congregation has its own distinct personality? That personality comes from the leadership. Churches that have a reputation of rich hospitality have it because the leadership has practiced that lovely characteristic. The early church was good at this. Acts 2:42-47 is a description of warmth, open homes and sharing: "They devoted themselves to the apostles' teaching and the fellowship, to the breaking of bread and the prayers …and day by day, attending the temple together and breaking bread

52

in their homes, they received their food with glad and generous hearts... And the Lord added to their number day by day..." They even sold things so that their brethren would have what was necessary. Their brothers and sisters were more important to them than any material thing. And these were brothers and sisters they had perhaps only just met. Was that one reason they grew so quickly? I think it was.

We as leaders in our churches have such a wonderful opportunity to set the trend of hospitality once more. Every time we read of how the early Christians were hospitable it was the leaders who were being described. Lydia was still wet from her baptism and the first words out of her mouth were "If you have judged me to be faithful to the Lord, come to my house and stay" (Acts 16:15). What a way to start walking with the Lord – opening your home to the church and to the preacher. She and her household had the blessing of hosting our brother Paul. Priscilla and Aquila kept Paul too and they opened their home for the church to meet.

In fact, the shepherds of the church are to be hospitable. "An overseer must be above reproach, the husband of one wife, sober-minded, self-controlled, respectable, *hospitable*, able to teach, not a drunkard, not violent but gentle, not quarrelsome, not a lover of money. He must manage his own household well, with all dignity ..." (1 Timothy 3:2-4). Doesn't that amaze you that hospitality is amongst the qualifications of an elder? Hospitality is so important it is listed with things like "able to teach" and "not a lover of money."

Hospitality is a command for all of us. Yes, I said a command. Hebrews 13:1-2 says, "Let brotherly love continue. Do not neglect to show hospitality to strangers, for thereby some have entertained angels unawares." And I Peter 4:9 says, "Show hospitality to one another without grumbling." We as preacher's wives have such a great opportunity to model this for our church family. Our homes are not ours; they are God's. He expects us to use whatever He gives us for His glory. How are we using our homes for the kingdom?

The Shunamite widow knew how to prepare for hospitality. At first, she just fed the prophet Elisha. After she had been providing him with food she said to her husband. "Let us make a small room on the roof with walls and put there for him a bed, a table, a chair, and a lamp, so that whenever he comes to us, he can go in there" (2 Kings 4:10). We all need food and rest. The widow knew that this man of God needed to be well nourished and rested for God's work.

Look around your own home and create a space where you can have guests stay. I spent many nights as a child sleeping on the living room floor or couch. My siblings and I knew that at any time we might have impromptu guests and we knew our rooms would be transformed into temporary Elisha rooms. My mom wisely taught us that this was fun and a privilege. So, we were very involved in preparation for guests and then in serving the guests once they were with us. Making tea, coffee, or a small snack were all things we were taught to do, and we learned how to converse and care for our visitors. What a blessing!

"I get "What the be that could happen"

I was speaking by skype to my daughter and granddaughter the other day. Her parents were preparing for guests to arrive. Ezri was sixteen months and already she knew when they were preparing to be hosts. She eagerly "helped" her mom set the tea or coffee things out and anxiously watched the plate with muffins or fruit bread her mom had made. She is learning hospitality already.

My husband and I are in the empty nest years now, so we have a guest room always ready for when someone needs a place to lay their head. It is wonderful to be able in an instant to offer a place for someone to rest. Be aware of needs in your church or at work. Be ready to offer a place. Soon people will know you are willing, and you will have requests for help when others need it. If you can't provide a room, provide a place for tea or coffee. Food isn't necessary for hospitality. Just open your home for people to come and talk. Take small steps and build up to meals and rooms.

I love to think of biblical examples of hospitality. It helps me to keep doing what I should do. Abraham offered food, rest and conversation to many. I think of the time he hosted the three strangers in Genesis 18:2-5. "He lifted up his eyes and looked, and behold, three men were standing in front of him. When he saw them, he ran from the tent door to meet them and bowed himself to the earth and said 'O Lord, if I have found favor in your sight, do not pass by your servant. Let a little water be brought, and wash your feet, and rest yourselves under the tree, while I bring a morsel of bread, that you may refresh yourselves, and after that you may pass on-since you have come to your servant." He honored them verbally, saw to their physical needs and made sure they were fed. What an example of using what he had to welcome people even when living in the middle of the desert in a tent.

Others who I love to think of are Mary and Martha who opened their home to our Lord; Lydia who welcomed Paul and the fledgling church; Abigail who provided a sumptuous picnic for David and his men; Laban and his family who welcomed young Jacob who was on the run from his angry brother; Elizabeth who provided a place for a young unwed mother to stay before she faced the great challenge of being our Lord's mother. In many ways our affluence has allowed us to separate ourselves from each other. We no longer sit on the verandah in small houses where we can see and talk to each other. So, we will have to be a little more creative in making ways to connect with those around us in need.

My siblings and I grew up in a home constantly filled with guests. Our home on the mission field was a hub for the church. We saw hospitality modeled in our home. This example proclaimed by actions that we were trying to be the family of God. I believe we were a light. Mom was happy to share whatever we had with whoever we kids dragged home with us. She served lots of bread and gravy or pancakes – inexpensive but warm meals. She planned hospitality opportunities too. She often invited new or prospective Christians over for a meal along with mature Christians. This pairing was a good chance for the new and the mature to interact and help one another.

There are so many different ways to open your home to others. Here are a few I have seen used. Open your home for Bible study or church services. Paul says in <u>Romans 16:3-5a</u> "Greet Priscilla and Aquila, my fellow workers in Christ Jesus, who risked their necks for my life… Greet also the church in their house." I remember arranging chairs in our living room for morning worship in Mutare, Zimbabwe. What a great blessing we Mitchell kids had in seeing our family open our home for the church. Small groups, ladies' studies, youth devotions, and men's studies can be held in our homes.

Offer your home as a place for personal Bible studies. Maybe you are not ready to teach, but you could offer your home and offer to be a silent partner at the study. Offer a family game night, have everyone bring snacks (that spreads the burden of food prep); invite friends to Sunday lunch and when they offer to bring something …say YES. This helps them feel needed and part of the event. Invite friends over for breakfast at supper. This simple meal is one everyone can help with and is inexpensive too. Each time try to invite people not in your usual circle of friends. Extend the reach to those you are praying to win to the Lord. Often people will come eat with you before they might come for worship. Work towards that but ease the way with hospitality.

Practical Hints and Ideas

You and your family will be so blessed by hospitality. My grandma Taylor told me "always be hospitable and you will keep a clean house." She was very right; having guests over has helped me keep a cleaner home. You teach your kids this virtue without even thinking about it. It is modeled. That is the most powerful teaching tool. You help those you invite to know God; your example teaches other families how to be hospitable, and you have more time to talk about what is most important. There is not enough time after worship to talk with people and grow to know what their needs are. We must create more time to know them. Open your home. It will bless all.

Make your guest feel at home. Let them help with meal preparation, show them where to find water glasses. Show them where books and magazines are. Show them where the tea or coffee is so they will feel free to make it when they want it. The Mark Blackwelders host us at Freed Hardeman University lectures nearly every year. Their two children gave up their basement bedroom, den and bath for us and three preachers. They have a small hospitality bar in the basement. It has a coffee maker, microwave and mini fridge stocked with snacks, fruits, sausage and biscuits ready to heat. Their children who are now grown were cohosts with their parents. Those two young people got very excited to be hosts to so many who came to visit the family. We have always felt it was a home away from home because they as a family have been relaxed and help us feel free to be one of them.

One of the biggest things to remember when being hospitable is to KISS: Keep It Simple Sister. To end with, I have included here some really simple recipes that I have used many, many times when having guests in our home.

Quick Coffee Cake
1 ½ cups flour, 2 ½ tsp baking powder, pinch of salt, ½ cup sugar, 1 egg, ¾ cup oil, ¾ cup milk.
Use a whisk and mix. Pour into greased 8x8 pan or double and pour into greased jelly roll pan. Add topping and bake at 350 till golden. About 20 mins (Add chopped or whole pecans if desired).
Topping: 1 ½ Tbsp flour, 1 ½ tsp cinnamon, 1 ½ Tbsp oil, 1/3 cup brown sugar. Mix and sprinkle over batter.

This is quick and so aromatic. I often use it when I have sudden guests or as a quick dessert on Sunday. It can bake while you eat lunch. The aroma fills the house with the most wonderful, welcoming scent of cinnamon.

Donna's Hot Chicken Salad
2 cups cooked chopped chicken, 2 cups cooked rice, 1 cup chopped celery, 3 diced hardboiled eggs, ½ cup mayonnaise, 1 can cream of chicken soup, 1 Tbsp lemon juice, ¼ cup chopped onion, 1 tsp salt, pepper, 2 Tbsp dry parsley.
Mix together and put in 9x13 casserole dish. Cover with crispy rice cereal. Bake 30 mins at 375F.

This was my mom, Donna Mitchell's, dish. I usually double it as she did because we always have many eaters. It heats up well too. A light dish that green salad and any vegetable and bread can be added to.
My aunt Charlotte, who is the queen of hospitality, told her daughter-in-law that hot bread added to any meal makes the meal more special. So, I will give you my mom's roll recipe and biscuit recipe. One is quick; the other takes a few hours to rise but is also very simple and easy. Practice on your own family. They will love you for it.

Air Buns

½ cup warm water, 1 tsp sugar, 1 Tbsp dry yeast. Put in large bowl and let sit 10 mins until it bubbles.

Add: ½ cup sugar, ½ cup softened butter, 1 tsp salt, 2 Tbsp white vinegar, 3 ½ cup warm water. Gradually add 8-10 cups flour. Knead well. Dough will be very sticky. Grease top and cover with cloth. Let rise till it doubles, about 2 hrs. Punch down. Let rise 1 hr. Punch down again. Grease hands and form dough into egg sized balls. Place on greased baking pans. Let rise till it doubles again. Bake at 400 till golden. About 12 mins. Brush with butter.

I often use two cups whole wheat flour in this recipe now. Just to make it "healthier."

Mom's Biscuits/Scones

2 cups flour, ½ cup butter, 2 tsp sugar, 1 tsp salt, 4 tsp baking powder, ¾ cup milk or 1 cup buttermilk.

Blend all dry ingredients in large bowl. Cut in butter till fine crumbs. Add milk and blend. Knead two mins or until it has a satiny feel. Roll out thin and fold over. Roll again slightly. Cut out and place on greased pan. Bake at 450 about 12 mins. Rolling thin and folding over helps them split open nicely after baking. I double this recipe as everyone likes leftover biscuits....

I like to do High Tea and use these for scones, jam and cream. Slice scones in half and top with a spoon of jam and a dollop of real whipped cream.

Butter Dips (a quick and easy biscuit bread stick, good with spaghetti or any soup)

¼ cup butter, 1 ¼ cup flour, 2 tsp sugar, 2 tsp baking powder, 1 tsp salt, 2/3 cup milk.

Heat oven to 450. In square 9x9 pan melt butter in oven. Remove pan from oven.

Measure flour, sugar, baking powder and salt into bowl. Add milk; stir just until dough forms, about 30 strokes.

Turn dough onto well-floured board. Roll dough around to coat with flour. Knead lightly about 10 times. Roll into 8-inch square. With floured knife cut dough in half, then cut each half into nine 4 inch strips. Dip each strip into melted butter, coating both sides; arrange strips close together in 2 rows in pan. Bake 15 mins or until golden brown (I double this and use two pans).

Betty's Microwavable Vegetable Soup (serves 6-8)

3 slices bacon chopped small, ¼ cup chopped onion. Place in large microwavable bowl and cook on high 3 mins. Add 1 cup chopped celery, 1 cup thinly sliced carrots, 2 cups potatoes cubed small, 3 Tbsp flour, 3 cups V8 or tomato juice, 2 ½ cups water, ½ tsp dried thyme, 1 cup beef bouillon, salt and pepper. Cook on high till potatoes are cooked through. About twelve mins. Then add 1 ½ cups frozen peas, added five mins before serving.

I often cook this on the stove top. I like it because it is quick and light. Betty was my mother-in-law and a gracious host and example to me too. She has now gone on to her reward, but her memory still teaches.

Fiona's Chocolate Crunchies

1 cup oats, 1 cup flour, 1 cup coconut, ½ cup sugar, 1 tsp baking powder, 2 Tbsp cocoa. Mix all together. Add 6 oz melted butter. Mix and bake at 350 for 20 mins in an 8x8 greased pan. Top with icing while hot. Cut into squares as they cool.

Icing: 1 cup powdered sugar, 2 Tbsp cocoa, water.

Fiona is one of my childhood friends. She and Nigel are so gracious and hospitable. I double this recipe and press it into a jelly roll sized pan.

Kathy Goben's Crock Pot Pizza
1 lb hamburger, browned (she uses ½ hamburger, ½ sausage).
1 small onion chopped and cooked with the meat.
1 small bag (8 oz) rigatoni pasta cooked.
16 oz shredded mozzarella.
2 small cans pizza sauce (make your own by adding Italian seasonings and powdered garlic to cans of tomato sauce)
1 can mushroom soup
1 pkg pepperoni
Layer ingredients into greased crock pot 2 times starting with hamburger/onion, noodles, cheese, mushroom soup, pizza sauce and pepperoni. Top with cheese. Good with mushrooms and black olives on top of meat. Cook on low 4 hrs.

Make this Sunday morning, add green salad and garlic bread and you have a super meal.

Kathy and her husband Randy are members of the Winfield, Ks church and always open their home to all.

Fruit Crisp (I double this in a 9x13)
4 cups apples sliced and pared or any fruit. I like to mix frozen berries and peaches.
2/3 cup brown sugar...
½ cup flour...
½ cup oats...
¾ tsp cinnamon...
¼ tsp nutmeg...
1/3 cup butter...
Heat oven to 375. Grease 8x8 pan. Place fruit in pan and top with blended remaining ingredients. Top with pecans or walnuts if you wish. Bake 30 mins or until golden and fruit is tender. Serve warm.

I always keep frozen fruit on hand to do this. It was originally an apple crisp recipe, but we like the berry type now. Good offering for those with diabetes. You can use agave nectar and it would be even better for diabetics.

Questions

1. What does Acts 2:46 suggest about the first century church with regard to hospitality?

2. How could we have an Elisha room today? Read 2 Kings 4:10.

3. Mary, Martha and Lazarus made hospitality a family affair. How can we teach our children this virtue?

4. Describe how we could use hospitality to be evangelistic today.

Chapter 8: Ministry While Wounded

Death, illness, injury, family troubles – these happen in everyone's family and the ministry family is no exception. How do you continue to serve others while you are in pain?

Our family has had a particularly difficult year. My mother-in-law was put on hospice in January, my older brother died of a sudden heart attack at age 62 in February, my mother-in-law died in early April and in May my husband had a heart event and heart catheter later, after over a year of not having a lot of energy. To top it all, my younger brother reached a crisis point in his yearlong battle with colon cancer and had an 18-hour surgery with chemotherapy following that. And our daughter's son is in year three of his battle, at age 6, with leukemia.

When I read that list, I am exhausted physically and spiritually. I will share a verse that has kept us going: Exodus 14:14 "The Lord will fight for you, and you have only to be silent." Learning how to step back and be quiet and let God heal you is a challenge but is so very good. He knows what is best for us. He will bring to us exactly what we need, when we need it.

When our grandson, Ever, was diagnosed two plus years ago, it was amazing to us how God brought the things and the people we needed in that terrible time. Our daughter and her family live in the same town as we do and worship with us. People gave money, gift cards, food, babysitting, house cleaning, a shoulder to cry on, Starbucks… We were immobilized by our shock and grief. We felt overwhelmed, but God sent what we needed. God had even put our daughter's family only forty-five minutes from a children's hospital that specialized in Ever's particular leukemia.

Psalm 46:10 says, "Be still and know I am God." This verse has helped me through both my parents' illnesses in 2002 and 2014, and this year I have sung and said that verse over and over. Once more God asks us to stop and let Him do the work for us. We tell those we are helping to let us do things for them so they can cope, but it is harder to let someone 'do' for us. The helper role is far more comfortable than the role of the one in need.

God provided a study in our ladies' class that has strengthened me too: Rosemary McKnight's book *Those Who Wait*. Isaiah 40:31

says, "They who wait for the Lord shall renew their strength; they shall mount up with wings like eagles; they shall run and not be weary; they shall walk and not faint."

It is amazing that God had helped us choose a study that reminded me every week to wait, wait, wait on God to provide. This class, our weekly opportunities to worship with our church and my daily reading from God's word have been key to keeping me from giving up. In fact, giving up just never was a consideration because we knew that keeping nourished in the word and fellowship would get us through.

I think when you have seen others survive terrible loss you know you, too, will make it. The hard thing is being patient with how long this process takes. We want instant gratification in all areas of our lives, especially as a culture. So, it is ingrained in us to want instant gratification even while grieving, suffering illness or enduring other heartbreaks. Another verse, "Casting all your anxieties on him, because he cares for you" (1 Peter 5:7) has rung in my heart all year. Once more God tells us to give it to Him. God is God. I am not.

We know we need to give our troubles to God, but often we forget that we only have so much emotional and physical energy. This year my husband and I have had to scale back our activities in order to let ourselves heal. We have already talked in this book about the value of simplifying our schedules so we can be able to minister. During a time of crisis, we need to let others take some of our load and we need to just say "no" to doing some things. Time to just "be" is so needed in times of stress.

This year, I have spent lots of time looking at photographs of my brother and rereading some books he wrote. It meant lots of bittersweet tears, but tears are so necessary. Didn't Jesus show that by crying with Mary and Martha! Allow yourself time to grieve and remember.

My mother-in-law was in decline for about 5 years before she went to meet our Lord. My husband spent time with her, taking her to medical appointments and just being with her. She loved getting a pedicure/manicure with me. This was time we might have spent doing more ministry with those in our church but for this season we needed to minister to her.

When we are sick, we often tell people to listen to their bodies and rest when needed. Our minds and hearts need rest too when we endure trying times. We need to listen to our emotional tiredness and give ourselves permission to do what our hearts need.

One thing that has helped me in times of stress is to swim. Exercise rejuvenates our bodies and our minds. Find some outlet — yoga, walking, running, anything that helps your body release stress. It will give you strength that you might not have known you were lacking.

We need time alone, but we also need our family and church. Galatians 6:2 says, "Bear one another's burdens, and so fulfill the law of Christ." Bearing each other's burdens is only possible if we allow others to know we are in need. So, open up and share how you are hurting. Put yourself in the other person's shoes. Wouldn't you want to know how your sister or brother is hurting so that you can comfort and help them? Allow them the honor of service. Speak up. Ask for help if you need it; if you need space; if you need company; if you need your house swept....

Reading good books, blogs and articles about grief has helped me keep moving through the process of grief and reminds me others have wisdom that I need. In fact, I search out books on grief almost as if finding someone else's words about grief will bind up my wounds. These books often share scriptures and routines that have helped me cope with the sorrow and adjustment to the new normal. I will share some of the titles of good books on grief at the end of this book.

Illness, whether it is chronic or acute may also affect our ability to minister. I have diabetes and have had times when my back problems kept me immobile and even in bed when my kids were little. Navigating chronic illness might be harder than an acute illness. We all seem to have understanding and patience with acute problems, but after a certain amount of time people think you should be "all better." This is where being strong in yourself must come into play. Don't go beyond what your illness can handle. You will end up even more ill and resentful on top of it.

One other way I have found to help is that my husband and I use each other as a safety net. We don't say yes to an event without checking with each other. That's a good idea for not double scheduling but it has also enabled us to remind each other when we are over committing ourselves in busy or hard times. That's another way you can navigate ministry when wounded.

Remember — struggles and disappointments in life often occur when we have unrealistic expectations. If we think we can minister without sorrows and tough times, we are setting ourselves up for difficulty. Instead, we must arm ourselves. Prepare for hard things by building our spiritual selves up now in readiness for what lies ahead.

Our son, Chris Wheat, is a minister and was particularly close to my brother who died suddenly this year. The article he wrote for his blog after losing Stan is particularly good and helped our whole family as we dealt with the new normal. I hope it is helpful to you.

2 Cor 1.3-6

Waves of Grief

Have you ever gazed at ocean waves for a time? That's not necessarily my favorite pastime, but I have often found myself mesmerized by their movement. Maybe we can learn something from them...

My family is going through tremendous grief right now. We feel it an unnecessary loss because, in our estimation, it happened way too soon. So, we deal with grief in unique and very personal ways. Mine has been sporadic, slow acting, and sometimes visceral in its cruel trickery. Don't worry, I don't blame God for this. I know He can easily handle my wrath and confusion, my limited explanations and futile knowledge, but I'm already certain He is teaching me new lessons, and there is grander purpose than I can now comprehend in His designs (Isaiah 55:8-9).

No, I think the waves of grief are quite meaningful. You can wade out into them and find a variety of experience. Some will barely move you as they gently splash your leg. Some will make you jump just to keep your head above water, and some will take you down and roll you many times before letting go. If you try to fight them, they become your master, enslaving you to emotional outbursts at unintentional provocation. But if you should choose to ride them...? Some will take you gently back to shore. Some will train you to keep better balance, and some will take you farther than you can imagine, to a very enjoyable place and peaceful state of mind. At least that's what I've experienced so far.

We can be quite unrealistic in moments of despair, like David wanting to take Absalom's place, who died trying to steal his father's kingdom (2 Samuel 18:31-33). But David knew when to stop grieving as well (2 Samuel 12:15-23). I'm not talking about getting back to "real" life and staying busy so much as finally recognizing, however long it takes, that I won't see my friend again till God is ready to take me home. Some of God's most beautiful promises are made to those hurting and suffering. Paul gave such encouragement while sharing God's promise that *Christian* grief is different (1 Thessalonians 4:13-18). We have HOPE! We get to see our sisters, brothers, fathers, and mothers, in the Lord. And, even greater, we get to see the Lord Himself. Do you suppose the Savior can also handle these worries and fears? (1 Peter 5:7)

So, please my friends, ride those waves wherever they go, all the way to glory.

Chris Wheat

Questions

1. What are some ways you have been able to continue to minister while you were wounded?

2. Think of some ways to allow others to carry your burdens as spoken about in Galatians 6:2. "Carry each other's burdens and so fulfill the law of Christ."

3. "An anxious heart weighs a man down, but a kind word cheers him up" (Proverbs 12:25). Find someone whose words will hold you up in tough times big or small.

4. Pray God will help you to balance your workload so that "wounded" times won't burn you out. Schedule time every week to rest and recuperate.

Psalm 125:2
As the mountains surround Jerusalem so the Lord surrounds His people from this time forth + forevermore

Chapter 9: Trusting God for Tranquility

When I speak or teach women, one thing they all tell me they struggle with is finding peace in their daily walk. We cannot be intentional women when we are in a state of turmoil.

Do the following words describe you and your life? Agitated, worried, discontented, angry, easily "ticked," aggressive, complaining, grumbling, dissatisfied? As preacher's wives we are often the first person someone remembers or meets at a church service. Whether we choose to be or not, we are in the limelight. Our attitude will often be equated with the attitude of the church.

This is true of any Christian as we are God's ambassadors but, especially as the wife of the preacher, we are more visible than other women. If the above words describe us, others and especially outsiders will think they describe our Lord's people.

One of the passages that I sing to myself almost daily is "Be still and know that I am God" (Psalm 46:10). I think we as God's women need to learn to be still. Just be quiet. We live in a frantic world. Everyone is harried and hectic and harassed. We need to learn to be calm and content. We need tranquility, serenity, contentment.

Tranquility is not something that just happens. We have to ask God for help in this area. We have to trust Him for that tranquility. I sang this song as I walked from the guest house I was staying at in Kansas City to the hospital where my mom lay preparing to leave this world for the arms of Jesus. She had been in hospital nearly two months. I had expected the final moments for weeks. It was amazing how just those simple words did calm me. I was looking in the right direction – God's direction. When we keep our focus right, our attitude will be right.

Jesus promised that in this world we would have trouble. And certainly, in ministry there are many troubles, ours and our church family's. God promised to enable us to have peace and contentment in the midst of trouble. The troubles will not be removed; instead, he will give us what we need to endure the troubles. John 16:33 says, "I have said these things to you, that in me you may have peace. In the world you will have tribulation. But take heart; I have overcome the world." God is telling us not to worry or fret. We are on His side and He has already won the battle.

We, of all people, should exemplify peace and contentment. We almost take an absurd pride in being able to "out do" each other in stressed out lives that are much too busy. We say things like "I am just so busy," "I don't seem to get everything done," "there just aren't enough hours in the day," or "you wouldn't believe how busy our schedule is." As if being exhausted, worn out and unhealthy makes us extra righteous! Why do we have to compete like this? We need a tranquility revolution. We need to get off the merry-go-round. We need to simplify our lives.

Most of us are trying to do too much and end up not doing any of it well. Wouldn't it be better to say, "I've lightened my load so that my family and I have time for God, for each other, for sanity, and now we do less but do it better and with more joy?"

Perhaps we need to memorize more verses like Matthew 11:28-30. "Come to me all who labor and are heavy laden, and I will give you rest. Take my yoke upon you, and learn from me, for I am gentle and lowly in heart and you will find rest for your souls. For my yoke is easy and my burden is light." He did not save us to burden us. He wants us to have peace from allowing Him to be our source for all we need. Particularly, I think we need to remember that He promises we will find rest for our souls.

There are several serenity thieves that come to my mind: loving material things, selfishness, ingratitude, worry, unresolved sin, and lack of forgiveness. Our lives need simplification in many areas. How we deal with these will shape our family, our ministry, and our hearts.

We are drowning in "things" in our culture. Often, we have to dig our way out of our cluttered houses before we can really say we have simplified our lives. Try this exercise and you will be amazed how "light" and peaceful you will feel. Go through all your belongings one room at a time and get rid of anything you have not really used or worn or read in the last six months. Be ruthless. It is such a cleansing feeling to be rid of things we just do not need. Taking care of all the "stuff" we have burdens us and uses up precious time and energy.

Perhaps the wisdom found in Proverbs 25:16 would help us to learn that we should be content with enough: "If you have found honey, eat only enough for you, lest you have your fill of it and vomit it." When we have too much of a good thing, it can make us sick.

Sometimes we need help in accomplishing this simplifying. Ask for help. Choose someone who will be honest with you – one who

What's the best that could happen?

can look at your daily, weekly, monthly schedule and point out where you are overloading yourself. Be humble and accept the correction. Proverbs 12:15 (NIV) says, "The way of a fool seems wise to him, but a wise man listens to advice."

We all know deep down what is not needed in our lives, what is most important and what we truly can handle. It is just hard to make ourselves do the hard things, the cutting back and eliminating. Writing out goals makes it more concrete and real. "Commit to the Lord whatever you do and your plans will succeed" (Proverbs 16:3 NIV). Pray for strength to do what God wants. Pray to be able to cut away the fat.

When my mom became ill in 2002, I was visiting her for her congregation's ladies' day. I had planned to spend one weekend and had packed accordingly. I ended up spending two months in a guest house in Kansas City with what I had taken to wear that weekend and a couple of other outfits my husband brought me. It was an amazing lesson in what I did and did not really need. I was quite content as I cared for mom in her last days. I was dealing with what was truly important: being with mom. "Stuff" was relegated to its proper position; it became secondary to loving and caring. Wouldn't it be good if we could take that same attitude and apply it to our daily lives?

Hebrews 12:1-3 encourages us to throw off the unnecessary so that we can focus on Jesus and run the race with endurance. Sin weighs us down. "Every weight" that the writer talks about might be all the stuff and activities that keep us worn down and unable to be really content with the life God has given us. We need to trust God: Trust that He knows what our life should look like, where we should live and what we should do.

When I am discontent, I am saying God has made a mistake in where He has put me. How dare I! He is God; He knows what is best. "Trust in the Lord with all your heart, and do not lean on your own understanding. In all your ways acknowledge him, and he will make straight your paths" (Proverbs 3:5-6).

There are many things that steal contentment and joy from us. We can let circumstances steal our joy. Instead, we should remember Psalm 118:24 "This is the day that the Lord has made; I will rejoice and be glad in it." This verse shows that our attitude is a choice. "I will" indicates decision. Circumstances do not have to dictate my disposition. Philippians is full of reminders of what God has done for us and how this should make us so very thankful and joyful. An attitude of gratitude is what we need every single day. Joy is that attitude which causes us to be able to take whatever problems and crises that confront us and rejoice in the fact that God can use them for His glory and for our good.

I love Proverbs 30:8b-9, which says, "give me neither poverty nor riches; feed me with the food that is needful for me, lest I be full and deny you and say 'who is the Lord?' or lest I be poor and steal and profane the name of my God."

As ministry families it is often tempting to look around at our church family and be discontented with what God has decided we need. This verse is a good reminder to be happy with what we are blessed with. Counting blessings is always a good attitude changer. When we remind ourselves (as God often had to remind Israel) of how much God has done for us, then our attitude does shift to gratitude.

We cannot be contented people when we have sin in our lives or an unforgiving attitude towards others. These are closely connected as our forgiveness of others is directly related to God's forgiving us.

The parable that speaks most loudly to me is the Unmerciful Servant in Matthew 18:21-35. I think we often have a hard time with contentment because we are like that unforgiving servant who was forgiven everything and yet he was harsh and unforgiving to a man who owed him, in comparison, a paltry sum. Matthew 18:33-35 says "And should not you have had mercy on your fellow servant, as I had mercy on you? And in anger his master delivered him to the jailers, until he should pay all his debt. So also, my heavenly Father will do to every one of you, if you do not forgive your brother from your heart."

The older I get, the more I see we need to give one another mercy. Give each other the benefit of the doubt when we think we were intentionally wronged. We are too quick to assume that hurt was intended, and we are filled with anger and resentment. Instead, we need to assume no hurt was intended. So often, I find out later they didn't realize what they said or did was taken that way.

How many times have we said something that just came out wrong? Forgiving each other is so important to our own forgiveness and our mental health. Be merciful. "See that no one repays anyone evil for evil, but always seek to do good to one another and to everyone" (1 Thessalonians 5:15).

Contentment is accomplished when we have taken care to be at peace with our sisters and brothers. Be proactive. "If your brother sins against you, go and tell him his fault, between you and him alone…" Matthew 18:15-20 outlines how to do this. Go first; do not delay. The longer we delay the bigger the problem grows.

Often it is a very small thing that has grown larger than the small thing it initially was. Don't let a chip grow on your shoulder. Go take the time to resolve the issue. This is not easy. There are two choices when someone has wronged us. Go talk to the person and try to make peace or quit whining about it.

As a preacher's wife I have had to make a choice about who I spend most of my time with. I have tried to steer clear of people who make me feel discontented and agitated. Instead, I gravitate towards those who help me become better. Proverbs 13:20 tells us "He who walks with the wise becomes wise, but a companion of fools suffers harm." Also "Anxiety in a man's heart weighs him down, but a good word makes him glad" (Proverbs 12:25). Spend time with people who will help us "carry" each other's burdens (Galatians 6:2). Be humble enough to lean on those who want to help you.

Worry is probably my biggest contentment thief. I know worry is a sign I am not trusting God to be in control. It is very hard for those of us who like to be in control to let God rule. But we must. Matthew 6:34 says, "Therefore do not be anxious about tomorrow, for tomorrow will be anxious for itself. Sufficient for the day is its own trouble."

"Yet you do not know what tomorrow will bring. What is your life? For you are a mist that appears for a little time and then vanishes. Instead, you ought to say, 'if the Lord wills, we will live and do this or that'" (James 4:14-15). These are good verses to print and stick on our mirrors or fridges where we can constantly be reminded to let God take care of life.

It is very hard to stop worrying and allow God to cradle us, providing for us like a good father. We don't usually worry about eternal things. The things we worry about are things that in fifty years will no longer matter.

Hope is what gives us the ability to be content. We have heaven to look forward to. We can trust God to provide that wonderful home. Keeping the vision of this home in our minds will help us sort out what is "eternal" in importance and what is not.

Questions

1. What does tranquility mean?
2. Do unresolved personal relationship problems interfere with tranquility? Read Matthew 18:15-20.
3. Worry steals our peace. What does God say about worry? Read Proverbs 12:25; Matthew 6:34.

Chapter 10: How Can the Church Help?

As I was thinking of chapter topics for this book, my wise brother suggested a chapter about how the church can help the preacher's wife and her family. There are many things in our lives as ministry families which have not been helpful. I will talk a little about those but will also try to share some things that those in ministry have told me they would love to receive from their church family, as well as some stories of good things they have received from the body of Christ.

First, please remember that we are battling against Satan, not each other. We are on the same side. We need to help each other on the journey to heaven. That means that we need to encourage and help the preacher and his family in their journey too. In Romans 1:11-12 Paul tells the church "For I long to see you, that I may impart to you some spiritual gift to strengthen you— that is, that we may be mutually encouraged by each other's faith, both yours and mine." What a beautiful sentiment! How can we help the family and the man who encourages and teaches us?

The body of Christ has many parts, not just the "preaching" part. If every part is working and doing what it should, the work will be evenly distributed. This will lift the burden of too much work from our preaching family. We need to see how wonderfully the body functions when all the parts are working.

Often the pastoring in our churches is left to the preacher. This is not their biblical job description. Not that it is wrong to have a pastoral or caring way of ministry but that the preacher should be concerned with the word and teaching instead of hours spent shepherding the flock. Strong elders are so necessary for strong churches. Let us pray that our elders will have courage and strength in the job of caring for the flock, taking that burden off the preacher's shoulders.

Elders should be a buffer against minor complaints from the brethren, not a conduit. Ministry families need to hear from their elders that they are needed and appreciated. They even need to see that reflected monetarily. When we underpay our ministry family, it hurts the kingdom because our minister has to constantly worry about how to make ends meet, instead of on how to preach and teach to the church and to the lost! We should pay him what other professionals in our congregation are paid. This is a man and wife who have often spent many years training and possibly incurred debt in order to be prepared for the Lord's work. We show that they are loved by taking care of their needs. I Corinthians 9:14 says "… the Lord commanded that those who proclaim the gospel should get their living by the gospel."

Don't make the preacher feel guilty about asking for a raise. Even a cost-of-living increase would be appreciated. I cannot count the number of stories I have heard of ministry families moving because they cannot make it on the little they are paid. Ministry families usually have to provide their own medical insurance and pay their own social security. A fair amount is needed to take care of those requirements as well as the ordinary cost of providing a home and food. Talk honestly with your preacher; let him share what he needs and how he would like his compensation divided out.

Communication is so vital to any relationship but especially between the leadership of a church and their ministry family. Often a preacher will leave a church without talking things out. The church is surprised that the man was unhappy. Create an atmosphere of trust where open communication is possible. Periodically open the conversation with the preacher and his wife about what their requirements are. Needs can change and this is vital to the health of the work of the Lord.

Churches need to make sure that the preacher's family has adequate vacation for rest but also time to rejuvenate and recharge themselves spiritually. Allow time for both the husband and wife to go to lectureships and seminars where they hear other teachers and benefit by fellowship where they aren't the ones planning and providing for the group. A full sponge is far more effective than a dry one. Let your preacher and his wife go "soak up" some good things for their strengthening, and it will have the added benefit of fortifying the local church on their return.

Our ministry families are usually hurt most by our words. I often hear sharp and unkind criticisms of the preacher, his wife and his kids. Truly unrealistic expectations are laid on these families. No one could be as perfect as we seem to expect them to be. We need a huge helping of mercy, kindness and compassion and then we need to shut our mouths. Didn't our moms tell us "If you can't say something nice, don't say anything at all!" This is good advice any time but especially with regard to our ministry families.

The same passages we teach our kids about the dangers of the tongue should be applied to what we say about our ministry families. "From the same mouth come blessing and cursing. My brothers, these things ought not to be so. Does a spring pour forth from the same opening both fresh and saltwater?" (James 3:10-11). How can we say we are Christians and then use our tongues to tear down and criticize our preacher's wife who is after all an unpaid and unpraised volunteer? Proverbs is filled with wisdom about how to use our tongues. "There is one whose rash words are like sword thrusts, but the tongue of the wise brings healing" (Proverbs 12:18). We should be using our tongues to give these precious families healing instead of "sword thrusts." They need our prayers and encouraging words, not stabs in the back.

It is amazing to me how long I can go on a simple thank you or small act of kindness. We had a group of gentle ladies in one place who would make us pies, send notes of encouragement or have us over to eat. It is amazing how being a guest and not a hostess makes you feel appreciated. One sweet lady made a whole meal and brought it over during a gospel meeting when we had the visiting preacher and family in our home. How wonderful to have a meal taken care of during a very busy week. In fact, she told us she was doing it because she knew how much we kept people and might need some help with food. One lady heard me say during our first year with that congregation how much I missed being spoiled by my mom on my birthday with a chocolate cream pie (at that point, Mom had died ten years before). Every year "granny" arrived with my birthday pie. That made our whole family feel loved and cared for. It was delicious pie too!

Preaching families do not get burned out because of preparing lessons and studying long hours; rather they get burned out by the nicks and dings inflicted upon them by members carping about things that should never hamper God's work. As with all our Christian family, they need encouraging words and kindness.

Elders, praise your ministry family publicly and privately. They need to hear you are pleased with their work and it is good for you to let your congregation know that you are proud of the hard work they do. This will set the example of encouragement and praise to the body. The body will then learn to use praise to the preaching family and to others in the body. Paul was so good at doing this.

"First, I thank my God through Jesus Christ for all of you, because your faith is proclaimed in all the world" (Romans 1:8). He was praising and thanking the Roman Christians in a letter that was then shared with all Christians. We should not hide our regard for each other. Praise all the time. It creates such a loving, positive, warm place for us all to grow.

Words and deeds should go together. Show your ministry family they are cared about through small acts of kindness. One preacher told of a family who offered to buy him a new suit. The preacher asked them to buy something for his wife instead. They had little money for new clothes. The couple took the wife shopping and then turned to the preacher and said, "now how about that suit for you?" They bought him two much needed suits and at a store the preacher could never have afforded. What a wonderful expression of loving appreciation. It was all the sweeter because it was so unexpected.

The same preacher told of a mechanic who serviced his car for free. We have been blessed by members who have "palmed" us fifty dollars telling us to go eat out and see a movie. Little gifts that say "we love you" go a long way to energizing our people to keep going. "So then, as we have opportunity, let us do good to everyone, and especially to those who are of the household of faith" (Galatians 6:10).

The ministry family lives in a glass bubble for all to see. Those families with children need the church to give those kids a break. Don't gossip and expect the kids to be better than our own children. Rather encourage and help them through prayer and a listening ear when needed. We had some wonderful "extra" grandparents in all the places we lived, members of the body who took a special interest in our children. They took time to praise them and find out what they were doing in school or hobbies. They especially took time to praise them when they were growing spiritually. What a help that is to any parent who is trying to train their children!

The biggest thing the church can do to help the minister's family is to let them be a real family, not some exalted, "set on a pedestal" family. Those expectations are unrealistic and unfair. Your minister's family is like any other family in the pew. They have daily struggles and will have faults and difficulties. Don't pick on them; be allies. Satan wants us to pick apart these embattled families. He wants to defeat us by getting us to fight our own soldiers. Refuse to let him win.

It's hard to be critical of someone you are praying for.

Questions

1. How does brother Paul describe the relationship between congregation and ministry person? Read Romans 1:11-12.

2. Does the Bible say preachers should be paid? Read 1 Corinthians 9:14.

3. Look at the start of these letters by Paul to churches and individuals: Ephesians, Colossians, I and II Timothy, I and II Thessalonians. How did he build up his brethren? What can we learn from this?

Practical Hints and Advice

Here are some practical hints and advice from preacher's wives I admire. I have tried to leave their advice completely in the way they gave it to me. Proverbs 15:22 tells us advice is vital for success: "Without counsel plans fail, but with many advisers they succeed." Much of what they told me, again, would be good for all Christian women to listen to. We all ought to be God's "priests" and workers in His vineyard.

- Husband – be aware he has duties. He needs time to study and prepare lessons. Just because he may be at home and not working from an office somewhere outside the home - wives sometimes distract him in order to help with her work.

- Perhaps the most difficult responsibility of the preacher's wife is to care for her family when her husband is away. He may be travelling in order to speak or he may simply be helping other people with their problems and trials. These things do not happen during normal working hours, and the wife needs to patiently go about her duties and be pleasant and loving when he returns, often weary and sometimes discouraged. She has to be willing to share her husband with others.

- Many will love him and depend on him; they will need him and call him at hours that may not be convenient to her. Alexander Campbell (early preacher in the restoration movement in churches of Christ) wrote of his mother, also the wife of a preacher: "I never heard her complain but rather to sympathize with him in his works of faith and his labors of love. She endured cheerfully the privations of his company in the full assurance that his absence from home and labors ...... meant glory to God and to the happiness of man.... She taught her children while he was away." Alexander memorized many scriptures and gave her credit for his Bible knowledge.

- A preacher's wife is her husband's teammate. All of her life is centered in being his helpmeet. She will keep an orderly home, can keep a confidence, refuse to gossip, accept criticism; have patience and show hospitality. What a joy it is to be married to a preacher! I would not have it any other way.
- Listen closely as he describes his plans for upcoming lessons and give good input.
- Listen well as he gives the lesson. (How embarrassing to fall asleep during your own husband's lesson!)
- Give him helpful feedback afterward. Don't just say "good job" every time. He wants to know specific examples of what I liked, what I thought was a powerful point, what I disagreed with, what I thought could be explained better, etc. He wants to get better at preaching and teaching and I'm in a great position to help him. * (tailor this to your husband's way of receiving criticism, some may be less able to take criticism than others)
- Another wife gave this advice about her husband's sermons. She said "Do not critique your husband's lessons. If he mispronounces a word, he is only human. Chances are someone is going to point it out to him anyway. NEVER point out anything like that in front of others especially."
- Always let your husband handle conflicts that come up in the church. It is easy for we women to become tools of divisiveness rather than healing. I would say "stay out of it."
- Choose your best friend carefully. She should be someone able to hold her tongue. Choose someone spiritually mature, maybe even someone not in your congregation.
- Pray daily for every member of your congregation.
- Young wives who are just starting out and feel the eyes of the brethren on her to see how she will 'perform,' just be a Christian, the kind God will be proud of, and you will be the best preacher's wife you can be.

- Visiting and having people over for meals is way more important than being able to speak publicly. Taking a meal to someone who is sick or caring for someone's children in a time of need is appreciated much more than being a top-notch teacher (and it is something all of us can do).
- Interviewing for preaching jobs is hard. Be yourself and encourage your children to be themselves. Try to keep the "pressure" of the situation from being pressure on them. Talk about God being the one who decides where we go as a family. Trusting Him for leading.
- If the elders ask to meet with both your husband and you, be yourself. Make a list of things you want to ask. This is a two-way interview. You and your family will have to "live with" the church you choose, so speak up. Be very positive about what you need and want. Don't speak disparagingly of other situations. Frame your needs positively. Be ready to tell the elders what you are gifted in and what you are willing to be involved in. Remember your primary role is wife and mother no matter what.
- One young woman described how her dad and mom would walk to the back of the church auditorium after the sermon. She thought for a long time it was her dad just wanting to parade her mom in front of the church. Her dad recently explained that it was wise to have his wife right next to him when women came up to greet who might be immodestly attired or want inappropriate attention from the preacher. Having the wife there is a good reminder that he has a wife and the wife often can interpret intentions that the man may not be able to read.
- It is wiser for women to counsel women as a general rule. If you are gifted in listening and counseling, step up and fill that role in your church. Titus 2:3-5 is a good passage to think of in this regard.
- My husband and I try to counsel together with couples, and certainly if there is a woman who wants my husband's advice, we tell her we will meet with her together. It is kind of like the idea of a nurse being present when a woman is

examined by her doctor. It protects both parties if there is a third party there. I would encourage any preacher's wife who feels she is gifted in listening and counseling to educate herself in this area. Read good Christian counseling books or even take courses when possible. Another way to equip ourselves for working in the kingdom.

- A challenge I face is "that one." There's "one" in every congregation. The person that complains bitterly but does nothing to change the situation. The one who wants to tell you all about the problem; that way, you can be the one to get in trouble if the change goes wrong. The person you duck into the lady's bathroom stalls to avoid. How do you handle that one?
- Bite your tongue a lot.
- Be very patient and give any congregation at least two years before you make any decision about moving on. If a preacher's wife can last and encourage her husband and family past the third year the longevity helps you to become a "part of the family" and perhaps you do your best work after that. By then you have been at babies' births, been at deathbeds and have held the hand of many suffering or sick. You have taught in the Sunday school program, provided many a covered dish, organized VBS and possibly hosted teen events. You have chaperoned Bible camp, taught women's classes and been to many hospital visits. You have helped your husband visit newcomers and encouraged others to participate. And the list goes on. That endears a preacher's wife to the "family" of God at any congregation.
- Smile.
- Understand your own talents and realize that you are part of the body. It's crazy to try to fulfill everyone's "expectations."
- Take a day off.
- Hospitality is not about straining your budget and tiring yourself out by running the sweeper obsessively. Often,

people just love an open door and ear and a cup of tea. Let your visitors feel "at home" by letting them be a part of the prep, like filling glasses with ice or setting the table. Or let them bring something to add to the meal. Let guests be family.

- Love, love, love your children. Help them understand they are children of the Lord and do not have to act any better than all the other kids. There are no special or stricter rules for preacher's kids.
- The most important "outreach" you do will be to win your own children to the Lord.
- Sometimes I feel the pressure, especially at something like a funeral, of being introduced as the preacher's wife. People you may not even know or have met yet latch onto you suddenly and parade you to all of the family. "This is the preacher's wife," they say, and then there is a moment when they all look expectantly at you. At that moment I feel nervous and confused. Am I supposed to perform? I realize then that I don't have to perform. All they really want is for me to be someone who takes the time to say something, to grasp their hand, to say "we're thinking of you."

Proverbs 9:9 says, "Give instruction to a wise man, and he will be still wiser; teach a righteous man, and he will increase in learning." We who are in ministry long to know how to do better. This verse says the one who is wise is wise because he or she asks for help. We want to increase our learning. I am so thankful others have walked this path before me and can advise me in my ministry. I hope these sisters' heartfelt words can help us all be better in God's kingdom.

From the Preacher's Kid: A Reflection in Two Letters

Let's face it. We are all SO different! A microcosm of humanity, and of the body of Christ. We're golden children, the black sheep, the strugglers, the loners, the old souls, the gurus and just about everything in between. And we should be! We reflect the Creation we're born into – one that is beautiful and diverse. For each of us, the label of preacher's kid (or missionary's kid, and all the variants) comes with a swirl of emotions and opinions. So, let me say it right now: my experience isn't going to match up with yours completely... but I'm so grateful we can share this for a moment and learn from each other.

Coming from a faith tradition that is steeped in Scripture knowledge, I always reach for whatever might be relevant to my audience when I'm asked to share or teach. There really isn't a chapter or a verse addressed to PK's, is there? There's a slew of reasons for that (and you're nodding probably), starting with the fact that ministry and church didn't look exactly the same in the first century. If you're like me – a missions kid (yeah!) – you can attest to the fact that while the beauty and power of the gospel is universal, and the teachings of Christ can reach any culture, the way various cultures "do" church is different even now. So, one or two scriptures for we who grew up saying, "my dad's the preacher", or "my mom is leading the Bible study"? Nothing direct. But that's okay... we have the whole Bible instead.

You might be reading this and nodding, you might be reading this with hurt and sadness, or maybe feeling distanced from this title. I think I have experienced all of those things and there are so many other feelings and memories attached. We're preacher's kids. For me, that means we've been witnesses, first responders, learning on the job, wise beyond our years, shock absorbers. We're proud of the hard work we see our parents do, that no one else really sees. We are heartbroken over the effects of sin and a broken world. We have learned early that the church is not heaven... it's a family full of humans who love God and are growing up together.

Some of us have had front row seats to how to become a Christian, how to participate in the body, and how to navigate those ups and downs. Some of us haven't. Some of us watched our parents struggle to meet a calling, and for whatever reason, ministry as a vocation hurt more than it healed. Maybe you were hurt in that process or felt alienated and second best while your mom or dad attended to church needs over family needs. Maybe you watched your family struggle with a time like this and overcome. Wherever you lie on that spectrum, I know life has already brought you a lot of insight and perhaps the ability to see the perspectives of others. It's a mixed blessing that I have personally grown from and am thankful for, with all of its challenges.

Watching your father preach from a pulpit every week and seeing your mother adapt to the work and expectations of various ministry situations from a young age is the normal. Showing up early to the church building, staying late for every question, meeting or baptism, or singing at every funeral or wedding is part of your everyday life as a PK. Like every upbringing, whatever your parents' livelihoods, you watch, and you learn. For better, or worse, you learn from your parents' work and choices and then you make your own.

So, what have I learned being born into a ministry family?

Humans Have a Great Capacity for Love

You see it first in the hearts of your family members who are called to ministry. Our parents have a passion for teaching the Gospel, for growing in their faith, and for fostering it in others. That servant hearted nature is a beautiful trait. I'm thankful to witness it among so many of my family members, generations back. Seeing God's love reflected in the choices of those who raise you is not unique to ministry families, of course, but the direction and intention of your family's work is a beautiful baseline. From there, you learn about the love others are capable of, and that family can extend past blood. Family can be built through the calling of faith, and from there you may learn that the human capacity for love flourishes in the church. It can be such a powerful thing to witness acts of kindness and true empathy. These examples leave an indelible mark on our hearts. We see them in the family of believers first perhaps, and then learn to recognize it everywhere. Most importantly, you learn to love well and wholeheartedly.

Humans Are All Fallible and Capable of Awful Things

Right alongside the joy and beauty of loving well, and being a part of this family of humans, is our struggle! As a preacher's kid, this is a front row seat situation that is HARD. When you have servant hearted, wise and generous parents who choose ministry, you see the brokenness of the world around you early, and not always in the places that are expected. Perhaps the first struggles and sin you witnessed were seeing the fear, pride or vanity that many struggle with in church leadership. Maybe you saw this struggle, the effects of sin, and the result of difficult choices in the people your family counseled. This is why so many of us become "old souls" or so "mature." We see how hard life can be, and what we're all capable of doing. This struggle is no respecter of persons; no one is exempt.

Redemption and real love are the most powerful forces in a person's life.

Back to that front row seat... or maybe, it's a pew. I saw it early. My mother's eyes filled with joyful tears as she saw a new friend, or child she'd taught in Sunday school, walk down the aisle and ask to be baptized. At that age, I had no way of understanding completely how powerful and transformative a simple choice like that could be. But I saw it in my parents, grandparents, and so many others. I saw it in that faith family swirling around me. I saw the struggles, all the pain, sadness and uncertainty that a person can wrestle with... and the change that could begin with the choice to seek God. Our Creator made us to love, and love well, and when we do that so much good can happen! As I grew up and made choices for better or for worse – I knew that love and redemption were there for me too.

Becoming a Christian Is a Lifelong Pursuit

It's a commitment to a cycle of struggle, growth and accountability that develops you into the person our Creator intends you to be. I can tell you right now about the day I chose to become a Christian, and how cold the water was in winter and what I wore when we all stood together and sang. It was a special day. It took me a while to understand this though – that was just day ONE. Thank God! That lifelong pursuit of an intentional life, guided by Christ, was modeled for me by my dad and mom. They chose Him long ago, and they've not been perfect the whole way, but they are being perfected. Praise God. I have had a front row seat to their lifelong pursuit, and that of so many. Watching and participating in this cycle of love, struggle, growth, and passion… it's not always easy, but I believe it's worthwhile. Knowing this has helped me approach so many things in body life with grace and empathy for others.

I Am No Better than Anyone Else.

Look, people get funny ideas. For one reason or another, there's this weird standard that we hold our ministry families to… and sometimes we preacher's kids even buy into it. We are under a little more scrutiny because our parents are more "visible" in the way they were called. As a kid, I was definitely a bit of a know it all. Especially when it came to Bible trivia and just, knowing stuff. Life is a marvelous teacher, and in my lifelong pursuit I've learned that I am not extra special for being a PK… but I do think my experiences are a gift. That's different! Isn't it funny though, how being in this position does give you a certain privilege? The privilege I see and honor most is that I have born witness to the work of Christ in others, and it has helped me see my brothers and sisters all over the world more clearly.

Even the Most "Perfect" Believer has Blind Spots and Faults

That church member who seems to have it all together, who is in leadership, or who seems to always have the best reaction and right words to say… they're susceptible to the struggle too. You've seen it and this is really hard. As preacher's kids, we bear witness to this dichotomy. We see people who are so mature and full of wisdom, but perhaps they lack grace for others, or struggle to forgive themselves… perhaps they struggle with understanding another's spiritual walk, and judge more harshly than they ought. This is so hard to see, especially if you are still young and developing in your own walk. Perhaps this person is, at times, your parents as they minister. As a child, this is so challenging, because your perception and understanding of what you see your parents struggling with is limited. We often get opportunities to extend love and grace to those closest to us in these cases. It's not easy, and if you've been in this situation or now recognize it as an adult… it's okay to grieve and be sad about it as you grow and work toward your own healing. Grace is a discipline we are constantly developing.

In reflecting on my 38 years of experience as a preacher's kid, there are more things to be grateful for than not. My mother knew what it was like to be in this position. She's certainly one of the most generous "old souls" or gurus I've ever known. She and my dad never lost sight of who I was, or who my brothers were. They were so aware of their calling to be parents, as well as to ministry. They made sure we were included in family decisions, and we found our own place in the family of faith where we could use our gifts. We were invited into their work and world, because they wanted us to know faith deeply. When they faced challenges, they didn't hide it, they talked about it and helped us frame and understand what was happening. It's always my prayer that I can do the same for my children.

In closing this letter to you, my PK friends, I want to remind you of those things, and extend them if they weren't offered before. You're seen, and loved, and while none of us is perfect, your perspective and insight are valuable. As an adult, I am thankful to have been raised in an environment where I was aware of the world around me and the struggle and redemption that faith could bring. That awareness has made me an empathetic person with deep roots, and while I'm in no way perfect, I'm really glad I get to be who I am.

The work our parents chose, whether for a year or a lifetime, shapes who we are. It is a unique part, but not all of who we are. My prayer is that we can take those insights and perspectives and allow them to shape us and become part of that cycle toward who our Creator means for us to be.

This Is for You, the Beloved Body of Christ

You are incredible. The diversity and gifts within the body of Christ is breathtaking! Our ability to love well and share the story of redemption with others, to embody Christ and his teachings is limitless. We rejoice and grieve together. We create family among us, and that is part of the redemption story that heals so many. I am a front row (or pew) witness to this – a lifer! I'm grateful. The church is never static or still, it is growing and responding to the needs of the world around her. When believers are working to be like Jesus and loving one another, there is nothing like it. It is joy. It isn't always easy, but there is a sweetness to the work I've seen all my life. Thank you for being that. Thank you for picking up this letter because I know that means you're here to learn and to love well.

So, brothers and sisters… let's talk about the preacher's kids. Put the little jokes aside about "those preacher's kids," and let's talk. There's no use in sugar coating it, friends. We don't always take care of our preacher's kids like we should. Every part of the Body is unique, and each member finds his or her own way. So, I submit this reminder to you, beloved: No two preacher's kids are the same. Nor should they be. All preacher's kids have dealt with unfair expectations, judgements and even a sort of isolation at times. In the same way that the role of full-time minister places unusual stresses and expectations (for better or worse) on a person, the same things can drip down to preacher's kids.

Just as you play a special role in the life of your faith family, the role of preacher's kid is special. We're as different as can be, but because of the calling our parents have answered, we do share common experiences. As a lifelong PK, and as a person who has been a Christian for 25 of her 38 years, I hope I can share some of the insights with which I've been blessed.

Remember that we've been listening to conversations and witnessing behaviors from the breadth and width of Christ's body, good and bad, from behind our mom's Sunday skirts for a lifetime. We've learned how to hold the emotional weight and strain of our parents' work, alongside the joy. We've seen them mourn and rejoice with all of you – even when it's hard. If you know an adult preacher's kid, and they're still part of a church family, ask them about their journey. I suspect that you will learn some new things, and that it might be a blessing to that person.

That perspective, from under the pews between Bible class and sermon, or while communion trays are being wiped down, or when we come home to hear that listening tone of mom or dad counseling and praying with another member... it's a special one. I'm thankful to have it. Over the years, I've lived in many places and been part of several congregations alongside my parents as they worked in ministry. At each place, we bore sorrows and joys. Just as you do in any family. At every church, there were always a few special people who saw me and my brothers and made room for us. They "got" us and chose to ensure we were included. They played a large part in helping us form a picture of what a healthy church does to keep their ministry families healthy and well supported.

As an adult, there are still peculiarities and odd expectations placed upon me occasionally as a PK. Those moments are always an opportunity for growth and conversation with church family. While there definitely have been times that I've been misjudged, or where a person has assumed things about me based on my parents' work or personalities, I have learned that the gifts of being a preacher's/missions kid are far greater. The perspective and special insight we have allows us to serve others in ministry well and provide support.

So, how can the church support, and learn from, preacher's kids?

Give Us Our OWN Seat at the Table

We see it all and have since we were young. That means if we're in a healthy place spiritually, we are the people you want in leadership positions in your church. We see and understand the demands of church leadership and service. We can be strong advocates for growth and for tending to the wellbeing of ministry families. We remember what it's like to bear those burdens and have some ideas on how to effectively support those called to this service. While not all of us have had the same experience, we may be able to anticipate needs and provide support. That front row view means that adult preacher's kids know the demands and trials, and also the joy and reward, of service in the church. Even if it's not a formal role, former minister's children have a voice that can be used to inform choices and meet needs. A lifetime of seeing all that the body of Christ is, means we are ready to seek the discipline and growth opportunity of leadership in whatever form that may take.

Recognize What We Bring to the Table – Good and Bad

Not all PKs are created equal because our experiences shape us all! We may have unusual spiritual maturity, but we may lack in other areas. Many ministry families move frequently, live without stable health insurance, and often have modest salaries. This means that many of us may be creative or frugal, but we may have serious anxieties around financial decisions or developing roots in a community. Our adaptability and wisdom, or our healthy family relationships may mean that we're also detached in other areas of our life. Like every human in this broken world, we need to be loved well for who we are, then nurtured and challenged to grow. Thanks for taking us along for the ride and loving us when we're weird.

Take Care of Our Families

We grow up with you but being a PK doesn't mean we're magically more mature, or that we're undeserving of grace. Whether we're children, or adults, we grow at the pace God has laid out for us, just like you. That pace might not match the ideas and expectations of all who know us. That scrutiny is hard to face at any age. It's likely that as we grow, we will differentiate from our parents (which is healthy and normal), and it may surprise some that we don't think or do things the same way. We love our parents and are proud of the work they do. Most of us are pretty fierce about protecting them when they come under unfair scrutiny. We also rejoice when our fathers and mothers find work in congregations that see their gifts fully and work to support and empower them to live up to their calling. This is the best gift for us. An environment where we are seen as children, and where we're heard as adults, is invaluable. One where our family's work and wellbeing is cared for and respected helps all of us do better.

See Us, and Include Us

Love us well. Love our families well, include us and don't hold us at arms' length because we need you. We need to see the fullness and joy of Christ's body, because we're bearing witness to all the hard stuff, and, while our parents may be amazing, strong spiritual guides, they cannot always be. We need multiple voices and guides along our path of spiritual development. We need you. Our faith becomes stronger because we see how this family works across all the places we've lived, the people we've known, the stories we've born witness to, and hearing and seeing Jesus in it all. The best memories I have of being a PK are of homemade meals, singing and playing in your backyards. They are of hearing your struggles and moments of redemption, of knowing you and feeling fully known. Every time you've celebrated a moment with me, or cried with me, I've been drawn closer to this beautiful body of Christ – our family.

The older I get, the more thankful I am for it all. The older I get, the more I also see the privilege of seeing the world the way I did and being formed as I was. Reflecting on what churches can and ought to do to support our ministry kids has made me grateful and keenly aware of the responsibility to serve and love others who now choose the work of full-time ministry. I think about this verse:

"If one part suffers, every part suffers with it. If one part is honored, every part shares in its joy. You are the body of Christ. Each one of you is a part of it." (1 Corinthians 12:26-27)

I am grateful to be a part of you.

Stefanie Wheat-Johnson (Nancy's daughter)

Recommended Resources

Brantly, Kent and Amber. *Called for Life: How Loving Our Neighbor Led Us Into the Heart of the Ebola Epidemic.*

Bouma, Mary Lagrand. *Divorce in the parsonage.*

Brecheen, Carl and Paul Faulkner. *What Every Family Needs.*

Burgess, Allen. *The Small Woman* (Gladys Aylward's story, single missionary to China).

Chandler, Lauren. *Goodbye to Goodbyes* (A picture book for children).

Cloud, Henry and John Townsend. *Boundaries.*

Dobson, James. *Dare to Discipline.*

Dobson, James. *The Strong-Willed Child.*

Eichman, Nancy. *Keeping Your Balance.*

Elliot, Elisabeth. *Keep A Quiet Heart* (Anything by Elisabeth Elliot is excellent).

Gariepy, Henry. *Songs in the Night: Stories Behind 100 Hymns Born in Trial and Suffering.*

Gerhardt, JL. *Swallowed Up: A Story About How My Brother Died and I Didn't.*

Gerhardt, JL. *Think Good.*

Hobby, Georgia. *Give Us this Bread.*

Johnson, Aubrey. *The Barnabas Factor: Realize Your Encouragement Potential.*

Lawyer, Zelma. *I Married a Missionary.*

Leman, Kevin. *Sheet Music: Uncovering the Secrets of Sexual Intimacy in Marriage.*

MacDonald, Gordon. *Ordering your Private World.*

Merritt, Dow. *The Dew Breakers.*

Lewis, CS. *A Grief Observed.*

McKnight, Rosemary. *Those Who Wait: Learning How to Wait on The Lord in an Impatient World.*

Miller, Erin L. *Fighting for Kate: The Inspirational Story of a Family's Battle and Victory over Cancer.*

Miller, Paul. *A Praying Life: Connecting with God in a Distracting World.*

Mitchell, Debbie Griffin. *Life's Shipwrecks – A Survival Guide.*

Mitchell, Donna. *Among the People of the Sun: Our Years in Africa.*

Mitchell, Stan. *Give the Winds a Mighty Voice: Our Worship in Song.*

Mitchell, Stan. *Will Our Faith have Children? Developing Leadership in the Church for the Next Generation.*

Pollard, Kathy. *Return to Me: What to Do When Loved Ones Fall Away.*

Sheldon, Charles. *In His Steps.*

Smith, F. LaGard. *Meeting God in Quiet Places.*

Souder, Joy Martell. *Where is Joy? Searching for Peace in a Valley of Grief.*

Ten Boom, Corrie. *The Hiding Place.*

Trent, John. *The Blessing: Giving the Gift of Unconditional Love and Acceptance.*

Good Blogs:
> www.ahopefullword.com
>
> www.amaryheart.net
>
> www.bobbygwheat.com
>
> www.healthychristianhome.com
>
> www.highergrounds.live
>
> www.overacup.org
>
> www.radicallychristian.com
>
> www.wattsupwithkids.com

Eutychus and You

(Acts 20:7-12)

My Name is: _____

Today's Date is: _____

Title of the Sermon is: _____

Time to Listen to God's Word!

Things To Remember:

1. _____
   _____

2. _____
   _____

3. _____
   _____

KEY WORDS

1. _____
2. _____
3. _____
4. _____
5. _____
6. _____

Use the back to draw a picture about the lesson.